The Warbird

Three Heroes. Two Wars. One Story.

TEXAS STAR PRESS

ISBN: 978-0-9980614-7-4
LCCN: 2016914322

For every service member with a story to tell

Contents

Honors and Reviews

- *2017 Gold Medal, Independent Publisher Book Awards*
- *2nd Place, Literary Non-Fiction, Colorado Independent Publishers Association*
- *2nd Place, Military History, Colorado Independent Publishers Association*

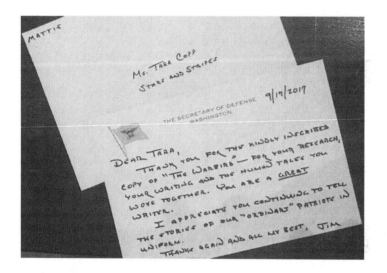

"Tara Copp has written a gorgeous memoir. Her firsthand experience of modern-day warfare is stunningly rendered, and the book has the drive and urgency of a great novel."

- **HELEN THORPE,** author of TIME Magazine's 2014 non-fiction book of the year, *"Soldier Girls: The Battles of Three Women at Home and at War."*

"Tara Copp is a tremendous author telling an equally tremendous story. What *THE WARBIRD* has accomplished is something that will resonate with veterans of all conflicts, all with a story to tell."

- **USAF COL. JEFF BRETT**, author of *"The 448th Bomb Group (H): Liberators over Germany in World War II"*

"Tara Copp's *WARBIRD* is an exhaustively researched war story, moving family memoir, and journey of self-discovery rolled into one - and it succeeds brilliantly on all counts. Written with a seasoned journalist's eye for detail, and a storyteller's narrative flair, it gripped me from start to finish. I outright love this book."

- **JEROME PREISLER**, *New York Times* bestselling author of *"First to Jump: How the Band of Brothers was Aided by the Brave Paratroopers of Pathfinders Company"*

"*THE WARBIRD* is a piercingly honest account of life in the war zone - both overseas and at home. Tara Copp shares her life as an 'embed,' measuring the toll of battle in blood and emotion as reporters struggle to transform the fury of war into a rational stream of words and images."

- **JIM DEFELICE,** #1 New York Times bestselling author of *"American Sniper," "Code Name Johnny Walker," and "Fighting Blind"*

"What did you think when you went to war?" This question is at the center of "THE WARBIRD." Connecting her own journey with her grandfather's six decades earlier, Tara Copp's engaging book takes you from Iraq to World War II and back. You'll learn about both, but most importantly about the enduring human story behind conflict."

- **P.W. SINGER**, author of "*Ghost Fleet: A Novel of the Next World War* "

"Tara Copp 's writing made WWII come alive as she draws the reader into the story line as if they were a participant with the subjects. Reading how she portrayed my Mother, Rose Monroe (AKA "Rosie-the-Riveter") was as if she had lived Mom's life story herself. To place one's self into the life of another so accurately is truly a gift. Thank you Tara for your wonderful, can't-put-it-down book!"

- **VICTORIA K. CROSTON**, Rose's daughter

"*THE WARBIRD* is a wonderfully written story of a young man's improbable ascension to B-24 bomber pilot and WW II hero. Far from the usual bio or war story, Tara's experiences with the heartbreaking calamity of war became an avenue to grapple with her grandfather's less-than-heroic impulses, which often paralleled her own post-Iraq struggles. Reflections on fear, camaraderie and feelings of desolation are so openly shared as to be disarming. I was quite taken by this book. It is a very intriguing story of restless lives, affected by war, in an unyielding world."

- **ALLEN BENZING**, B-29/B-24 Squadron, Commemorative Air Force

"'We sat in our stink and wondered at the speed of connectivity under a clear night of 1,000 stars.' Join Tara Copp as she invites you along on the journey to know her grandfather's war. Copp, an embedded reporter in Iraq, leads you through her own generation's war along the way, and the road through both conflicts is adrenaline-laced, deftly-written, and raw. This unique multi-generational perspective shows the harsh and derailing effects of war upon people's souls. It's a quest for redemption, for understanding, and it's a must-read for any pupil of combat nonfiction. The narrative, to steal Copp's words, is 'a wound up punch, waiting to land.'"

- **MARCUS BROTHERTON**, New York Times bestselling author of *We Who Are Alive & Remain: untold stories from the Band of Brothers*

1

The Warbird

E llsworth Air Force Base, S.D., 2005

The first time I held the photograph of the bomber, I didn't know what kind of warbird it was. The pilot, my grandfather, had died more than 15 years before. There was no one else in the family to ask. All I had was what he'd left behind: albums full of pictures, his World War II memoirs and a few extraordinary news clippings.

The photo was an oval-shaped Kodachrome print tinged

yellowish-green with age. It was shot on a cloudless day, by someone on the ground as my grandfather flew 500 feet above, holding his wings straight and level for a crisp keepsake.

I ran my finger down the bomber's lines. This was not a pretty airplane. Its nose was strong, bulbous plexiglass. It had four propellers and two side-by-side tails shaped like the souvenir pennies pressed flat at carnivals. The bomber's belly was fat, like a bloated fish.

I had pulled the photo from a family album during an earlier visit to my grandparents' home in California. At the time I'd just returned from reporting on Operation Iraqi Freedom. I came home understanding less about war than I thought I knew when I first went in, and I looked to my grandfather for help. Even though he was gone, he wasn't. He was in every wall of their home, in photographs of their life together, in dinner conversations with my grandmother and in all our quiet moments.

So I kept the photo with me. It was a rainy-day task; my goal to find out what kind of warbird it was.

On a 2005 reporting trip to Ellsworth Air Force Base in South Dakota, his bomber found me. I'd traveled there to cover base closure and the community's efforts to defend its hometown fleet of supersonic swept wing B-1 Lancers. The long, elegant Lancer was the modern American bomber and a workhorse in Afghanistan and Iraq.

My grandfather's bomber, on the other hand, was on the cover of a paperback book in Ellsworth's air museum gift shop. The book was propped up by itself, in a section on the great warbirds of the past. From the display I could look out the gift shop window, at the towering nose and wings of the fierce B-1 named "Let's Roll."

All war is connected ... my grandfather nudged.

I recognized the old bomber's profile immediately; its bulky crouch, the two tails. I grimaced that it was stuck in a corner like a forgotten old man, left to watch the youngsters fight on the grass.

I bought the book and cried on my flight home as I read it. My grandfather flew the B-24 Liberator.

2

The Embed

A hmed Al Jaber Air Base, Kuwait 2003
      The need to understand my grandfather's war started
with a sandy convoy, four airmen from Texas and a Humvee
named "Linebacker 10."

Nothing inside the Humvee was forgiving. It was all welded right angles and rough metal joints. By 10 p.m., it was also pitch black. I'd been stuck inside this sand-colored truck for the last 10 hours. Every time I moved, I scraped something new.

The four airmen assigned to this ride were part of the 17th Security Forces Squadron from Goodfellow Air Force Base, in San Angelo, Texas. I was the Washington correspondent for their hometown paper, the San Angelo Standard-Times. Their command chose which men would go forward to pull security for a supply convoy into Iraq, and approved my request: Please let me go too.

It was March 26, 2003. Six days after "Shock and Awe." Our Humvee had idled, bumper-to-bumper, with the Army trucks lined up in front of us and behind us for the last 10 hours, just inside the gates of Kuwait's Al Jaber Air Base.

The base had been a hub of fighter jet activity for days, ever since the first warplanes and cruise missiles and the massive forward movement of U.S. ground forces had collectively undone Saddam Hussein's defenses and Iraq's Republican Guard.

Linebacker 10 was part of the next wave, a snaking line of 86 vehicles of fuel, ammunition, water and food meant to keep the front lines moving. But 10 hours in, we hadn't moved an inch.

From my back seat in the Humvee I quietly wrote in a brown suede diary I'd purchased to chronicle this war. I held it open, reflecting.

I thought of my grandfather.

What did you think when you went to war?

The last few weeks had been a confusing buildup. Friends would ask, "Are you scared?"

"No," I'd answer back. But that wasn't entirely true. I was scared. Because I was excited. And I was nervous that it showed.

5

It can't be right to be excited to go to war.

But I was. I'd just left the Kuwait Hilton, a sprawling, gated hotel compound south of Kuwait City that the military used as a headquarters to sort and assign journalists into deploying units. I was one of scores of hometown reporters with no combat experience who were patched into units in a genius Pentagon maneuver that ensured hundreds of soda- straw views of an enormous land invasion.

Hundreds of reporters filled the Hilton, piling up hotel bills and daily expenses as we got immunization shots and had our blood types documented, as we compared notes and waited for the call to depart. At night we would gather at one news outlet's hotel villa or another. Kuwait was a dry country, so most of the time, unless someone had obtained beers from one of the embassies, the lubricant of those first weeks wasn't alcohol. It was war stories. The sexier the better. The more seasoned of the group had covered Afghanistan and Kosovo. There were even Grenada-era reporters in the mix.

Then there was me, with nothing to add. In the days before departure I packed and re-packed in anticipation. I suspected this experience would be life-changing. I hoped I would become one of the reporters with a war story to tell.

Then war started without me, and without the men of Linebacker 10. There would be no sexy launch or obvious hero's journey. Instead, in this dark night of exhaust fumes and shortening tempers, I made myself small in the seat, looked at each of the airmen around me, and started to write.

There was Airman First Class Valentine Cortez, 21. "Movie star looks, is bald, driven and muscular," I wrote in my suede diary. Next, Senior Airman Daniel Holmes, 22: "Has a picture of Risa, his girlfriend, tucked under his helmet strapping. Smiles almost every time I see him. Overwhelmingly thoughtful." Staff Sgt. Chad Wurm: "28 like me, but already graying. A quick- witted, highly quotable smartass Texan. The leader of our Humvee."

What I didn't write: "Already the center of my attention." Last, Airman First Class Brian Kolfage, the youngest of the crew. He was a 6-foot-2 babyfaced 19-year-old with Hawaiian blue eyes, smart alecky innocence and perfect teeth, traits that made him Wurm's favorite target. One of the "Three Kings." The George Clooney movie about stealing back Kuwait's gold from Saddam Hussein in the first Gulf War was a favorite here, and Kolfage carried a white king chess piece for himself, Wurm and Senior Airman Josh Washington, one of their best friends in the squadron. Washington was assigned to another Humvee up ahead of us. While we idled, the guys held the chess piece and struck a pose for me.

"You know how the reporter is in the movie," one of them teased.

Yeah. In a tent, undressed and on her back, I thought.

"Of course," I said in a sharp, but friendly, reproach. "That's not me."

Cortez, Holmes, Wurm and Kolfage normally rode four to a Humvee. After they learned I was their plus-one, the guys spent some time arguing about where to put me. They decided the safest seat was behind Wurm, who was sitting front passenger, weapon out. I got Cortez's seat, which meant he'd spent the last 10 hours standing in the sun's hot gun turret.

And we still weren't in Iraq. The men in this vehicle started to obsess.

Wurm was pissed. This war was slipping away before his crew would have a chance to be a part of it.

Desert Storm only took 100 hours, he thought, reaching again for the radio to call up ahead to Staff Sgt. Todd Fuller, squadron lead. Why weren't we moving yet?

Kolfage was consumed with the tunnels.

Iraqi troops are surrendering only to hide weapons under their robes, he thought. They filled ambulances with ammunition. They had a network of tunnels under Iraq. We could be ambushed anytime, anywhere.

"I'm gonna find those tunnels," he baited Wurm. "You shouldn't have told us about that."

"They've got booby traps," Wurm responded. "You'll get your ass killed."

Holmes obsessed about sleep. He'd been up for at least 13 hours, behind the wheel of this metal beast for the last 10.

Cortez rubbed his very sore ass and sunburned neck, and wondered who had the bright idea to add me to the mix. Me, their embedded reporter.

He wasn't alone in that thought.

What am I doing here, I wondered. I'd lost the bravado gained in the weeks of buying supplies, the adventurous attitude built up during a cold "reporter boot camp" the military ran us through at Fort Dix, New Jersey. There I'd learned basic first aid and field survival techniques. I'd done everything to prepare, except to really think about what it meant to be at war.

What I knew was I was here to tell the story of these men. As they wondered what their war story would be, I started to obsess too: Would I be qualified to tell it?

Finally, at 10 p.m., the radio call went out and 86 vehicles geared into motion. We exited the airbase gates and pulled onto Kuwait's empty highways. Parts of the convoy stretched out at a clip of 30 to 40 miles per hour toward Iraq while others came to a dead halt.

On an open road with no one else on it, I thought.

"Once we slow down, it takes a while to get Slinky back up to speed," Wurm said.

We passed a fuel truck with an Army Humvee attached for transfer. The tanker's barrel was marked JP-8.

"You're loading it with fuckin' jet fuel!" Kolfage hollered as we passed. "Dumbasses."

It took hours, but our convoy finally snaked to the last Kuwaiti checkpoint before Iraq. We were told to kill the engine and wait. Kolfage and Cortez threw vinyl mats on the rocky ground beside the Humvee to force a fast nap. Our driver, Holmes, leaned on the steering wheel and went unconscious.

I thought, "I'd better go to the bathroom before we go into Iraq."

There were no bathrooms, of course. So I looked for private slope to pee. I wanted to find a girl partner for this humiliating adventure, but in the dark it didn't feel safe to stray too far from the Humvee. So I just got on with it and hoped no one was wearing night vision goggles.

All of us were jolted back into reality when the squadron lead approached Linebacker 10's front windows in a growling rebuke. "You are not stopping for little Timmy Jihad, you are not stopping to fight the people on the ground," Fuller warned, looking each one of us in the eye. "You will die before you get out of this vehicle."

The convoy started to roll forward again, toward spotlights and the final border gate.

This was it. We were really going.

Through the Humvee's dirty window I saw Kuwaiti soldiers clustered in twos and threes. They stared at us as each vehicle rolled through.

9

Without moving my eyes from the window, I felt around in my dust-covered fanny pack. I found the tube I wanted. Before we passed the final berm, I applied a coat of dark lipstick.

"Damn. No big 'Welcome to Iraq' sign," Wurm said. And we crossed into war.

***

Our ride into Iraq took five days. I ended up staying much longer than that, but no other time left as bright an impression as that first ride in.

Besides reporting for San Angelo, I also worked as the Scripps Howard News Service Washington correspondent for three other Texas newspapers: the *Corpus Christi Caller-Times,* the *Wichita Falls Times Record News* and the *Abilene Reporter-News.* I'd come to D.C. as a congressional reporter, covering Texas politics, the farm bill and the implications of the drought.

The bright, terrible morning of September 11, 2001, changed all of that. Instead of covering a Congressional picnic I watched the Pentagon burn. In those early moments of terror, my editors told me to head for the monuments. My assignment was to feed "man on the street" color into the stories spilling out from our wire. So I stood at the Jefferson Memorial and watched two tourists from Montana take each other's hands as somber witnesses to the Pentagon's rising smoke. I cherished a happy bump of hope when I gave my water bottle to a thirsty U.S. Park Service Ranger who had been left to guard the Washington Monument. Maybe there was good about this day.

Then I felt the blank look of pity cross a mother's face when I asked if I could interview her.

I had overheard her talking; she had a military son. "What do you think this means?" I asked.

You don't really know, do you ... she flashed. "It means we are going to war."

That October we did. I started writing more about the three Air Force and three Navy bases in my Texas military towns. I covered Abilene's B-1 bombers as they took off against Osama bin Laden in Eastern Afghanistan and its Lone Star flagged C-130s when those warbirds joined the fight. I covered Wichita Falls, as its Sheppard Air Force Base-trained F-16 pilots patrolled Iraq's skies in Operation Southern Watch. I was moved by the portside kisses of Navy families from Corpus Christi, when Ingleside's mine sweepers and its command ship also got underway. After months of this, I felt pretty confident I knew the military.

But the truth was I only knew them from a distance. I knew the military from the polite formality of the marble and wood halls of Washington hearings, from the podium backdrops of political campaigns and from the traditional news features at Thanksgiving and Christmas honoring those who served. I knew those troops were better than the politicians sending them to war. But I didn't know the military at all.

Then in fall 2002 the Pentagon reached out to newsrooms across the U.S., looking for names. Creating policy. Building what would be the largest program in DOD's history to get the media on its front lines. What we should wear. Who was responsible for feeding us. Rules on operational security. Newspapers, TV networks and radio stations submitted 775 names; more than 500 journalists went. Eighty-five of us were women. In February 2003, I boarded a plane for Kuwait.

***

Our convoy through Iraq in Linebacker 10 was a haze of 20-hour drives and exhaustion. It was awkwardness and distance of all the assumed stereotypes that filled vast hours of no conversation. It was bombed-out vehicles spotted with blood from fighting and the rusted relics of tanks hidden in bursts of sand from that war 10 years ago.

"Stick a few trailers on the side of the road, and this would look like Oklahoma," Wurm offered.

"Is this the Highway of Death?" Cortez asked. No one answered.

There was no guidebook on how to act during the heavy clicks when Cortez rotated the turret or when Wurm scanned the horizon looking for threats. There was no right thing to say when Holmes pushed and coaxed and smacked the dashboard of Linebacker 10, demanding that machine keep moving as we played out the worst scenarios in our heads: *Please Humvee, don't overheat. Not here.*

It was the guys, then me, trying bit by bit to relate to each other and mostly failing. After all, I was the elitist East Coast liberal media person who had no business being here. They were the conservative Southerners whose service got taken for granted but always answered the call to fight.

And yet we were all in this Humvee. The men wanted to fight for their country. I wanted to cover them. So hour by hour each side started to soften.

They learned about me, as I started to feel it was safe to share. No, I didn't think it was strange that I wasn't married. I wasn't sure if I wanted kids. That I was okay with that. Then, just to throw them for a loop, that I even liked country music.

Bit by bit I learned about them, too. Our country had not been in a major war for 10 years, and I didn't have a single friend who wore a uniform. In the pre-9/11 days — the late 1990s and early 2000s — it was hard to understand why someone would sign their life over to the military. There were so many easier ways to make money in the fast dot-com landscape of the time.

I realized that except for Wurm, I was the oldest one in the Humvee. Yet each of the men had more responsibility than I'd ever had. They were military professionals who frequently got mind-numbing, shitty jobs and did them, so they would never be the ones who allowed the "what if."

And Wurm ... he was the oldest of the group, with the salt-and-pepper hair, biceps and a depth that suggested he'd lived more than his 28 years. Bit by bit, he kept impressing me more each day.

"Keep the window cracked," he directed Holmes, who was driving. Holmes had started to roll it up, to block a wall of dust from floating inside.

"Why?" Holmes asked. "So we can shoot!"

It was a long ride broken with moments of camaraderie and awkward jokes and permission to light up a Marlboro from the Humvee's back seat. In those hours Iraq's unforgiving sun and fumes started to mute out the rest of life's extraneous noise. I had a boyfriend back at home, a "catch" by D.C.'s standards. He was someone I worked way too hard to be with. I stopped worrying about it. There was no point when faced with this bright, dangerous day. I stopped worrying about other things too, those layers of explanations and unwritten rules and "D.C. nice" and collaboration and group think and worry over my possessions. They all started to fall off like unnecessary, flaking skin. Or scabs. It was intoxicating. Actually, that's the exact wrong word. It was like oxygen.

It was the most alive I'd ever felt. That felt uncomfortable. You get this feeling from war? But introspection was yanked away by the awful lurches of the Humvee in a poke to remind us all we were in hostile lands, and to keep our heads on a swivel.

Two days in we made checkpoint one, Camp Bucca. In the

years to come this facility would be a nest of ISIS. That day, however, it was home to a gagging shitter I slunk off to use. I was all sweat and dirty underwear, and the first layer of scum on my face had taken hold. I decided to leave it dirty. For the first time in my life, there was no real point to being clean.

"Take cover!"

Shots off to our right. Jesus. I grabbed for my camera and the men jumped on their Humvee. We all strained to see the source. Someone yelled: *Drive, now!* This was not a secure checkpoint. Cortez jumped into the turret, Kolfage scrambled into the back with me.

"We're moving!"

Or ... not. Three hours passed.

Three hours. Who gets shot at and then stands still for three hours?

An 86-vehicle convoy with an uncertain chain of command, that's who.

Or, us.

"I'm so tired of fuckin' waiting," Kolfage complained.

"We'll most likely get mortared tonight. We need to dig holes in the ground," Wurm said.

"Mortars? That's some straight up field shit," Holmes said. "Looking forward to getting mortared, peanut?" Wurm asked, eyeballing Kolfage.

"Waiting. That's the main reason I am not reenlisting," Kolfage snapped back.

Another hour.

"I wish we would get mortared," Holmes griped, thinking that might get us moving.

We only had a half tank of gas left when we were told "the Air Force is on hold."

Insanity, I wrote in my journal.

By this point, the sun was setting. Were we still going to go? That didn't seem like a good idea. But we were lined up for fuel and one by one the trucks started moving forward, toward the exit. Ten feet, then stopping again, to idle.

As the vehicles slowly snaked forward they aligned with the setting sun. The low light turned Linebacker 10 gold, and made its bulletproof windshield shimmer in a blue-green mother of pearl.

"Could I take a crew photo?"

The guys obliged and climbed on the hood. Cortez stood by his gun turret with a proud and threatening grip. Holmes climbed up too, then tuned us all out and listened to his headphones. Wurm sat on the roof, gun across his lap, with just a hint of a wise ass smile under his do-rag and sunglasses. Kolfage rode the windshield, long legs splayed across the glass.

"First in!" They quipped. They were the first Air Force Security Forces team on the ground in Iraq, and they weren't going to let anyone forget it.

I clicked the first frame.

On the next, I handed my camera to a passing soldier, and asked the guys if it was okay.

Come on up, they said, and moved over to make room. *You're one of us.*

I pulled myself up on the Humvee hood and looked directly into the lens. As I did, the ill-fitting helmet the Army had issued slammed down on my nose in a painful dent.

Looking back on that photo though, the main thing you'd ever notice was my big, fulfilled smile.

***

"We're not going tonight. There's activity up the road. We're done with the route for tonight," Fuller told the crew. I didn't tell these anxious men that I wasn't disappointed when Fuller walked over with this news.

"We've got three friggin' companies of MPs, and we're not going?" Wurm challenged. But there was nothing more to discuss.

Instead, we looked at the Humvee. Option one, stay far from it, since it was a mortar draw. Option two, stay as close as possible, because odds were much higher that one of us might be crushed by another vehicle than hit by a mortar.

Somewhere in the dark we heard more shots and the heavy gunfire of the .50-cal. A few minutes later, another of the embedded reporters riding in this convoy found me in the dark.

"I'm going home," he said. "I didn't sign up for this."
He told me about his young kids and the risks he was unwilling to take because of them. I offered encouragement but I thought he probably knew I was judging him silently.

How could you leave? This was everything we ever asked for.
But he was already gone. I realized a switch had flipped. I was still an observer, but I was also part of it now. Iraq had so easily stripped away everything except who I was in this moment, and who the men were with me. I couldn't imagine being anywhere else. I had a new model of ideal taking shape in my mind, too. Not men who knew how to spin words, but men who could shoot, who were single-purposed, to serve their country. It was a simple and naive and beautiful refresh of the stale.

So I climbed as close as I could to the Humvee and the guys. Instead of eating on our own, we shared our MREs together. Kolfage broke out a cigar, and I lit a cigarette. Wurm dug deep and left us hurting with laughter in a tear of one-liners. I passed around my satellite cell phone so the guys could call home and send emails, and we sat in our stink and wondered at the speed of connectivity under a clear night of 1,000 stars.

***

Tallil. The first air base the U.S. captured in Iraq. We'd arrived in darkness the night before. As we drove past the blacked-out airstrip the moon passed between clouds and exposed a line of skinny, silhouetted men kneeling in surrender on the runway, hands on their heads.

There must be tunnels here too, I thought, shuddering.

Valentine, Wurm and a few others from Goodfellow's security forces team walked the property in the dark, their flashlight beams taped over with red film. They spotted a darkened building and searched inside, then waved the rest of the team over. This was home. We pulled our rucks and backpacks and boxes of MREs and water from the Humvee, stacked them on the inside to secure them and unfolded our cots for the night. But nothing about it felt safe. It felt exposed and dark and full of unknown. Despite our exhaustion and the heat I lay there, eyes open, pulling my sleeping bag to my chin. I worried about what would crawl on me, who might be walking around in the night. Somewhere in the worry I found moments of jagged sleep.

When we woke the next morning, we explored the base. We walked on what we hoped was a worn, safe path toward a small row of buildings. A helpful soldier who'd arrived the day before pointed out where they'd marked unexploded munitions and how to spot the ones they hadn't marked yet. To me, each pile of rocks looked the same. Dirt or stones then maybe a soda can and more dirt, all blending into miles of more sand, more rocks, and more discarded cans and trash. Except some piles were a lot more dangerous than others.

The first building we entered had dirt clay on the outside,

plaster inside and windows that did not open. There was a door frame, but no door, just a dirty sheet. Pushing the sheet aside, we stepped into the bizarre: an Iraqi soldiers' bedroom. Army intelligence was already inside, learning what they could.

Inside were six metal frame beds, but only a few had mattresses. The rest were just exposed wire coils. There was a coating of dust on everything, Tallil had been miserable with sandstorms. I leaned in to look at the odd remnants of life. There was a shelf with a bright blue pack of "Sumer" king size cigarettes and a sea-green plastic bunny-shaped soap dispenser. The window was covered by short pink curtains — that had flowers on them. At the sink, there was an orange heart-shaped towel rack and a used tube of "Sinan" toothpaste, which boasted in English of "classical taste, powerful effect." The small fridge still had brown eggs in it, and there was a duffle bag on the floor, a touristy bag from Branson, Mo., covered in images of cowboy hats, stars and mountains.

This is the enemy? I thought.

"Someone left here recently," the Army intel officer said. "The batteries in the clocks are still good, and the time is accurate."

Already rumors were that more than 100 Iraqi militants had been found at Tallil since we arrived. Under the runway.

"There's a whole tunnel complex under this base," the officer said.

I wasn't going to sleep tonight, either.

We went back to the sandy building the men had set up as a headquarters. Wurm boiled water and dragged a half bombed-out car, a rusted door and some netting into a pile. This would be our bathroom.

"We are going to have a restroom tonight. It's not going to have a bidet, but there's only so much I can do in one night," he said.

18

"What about a ladies' room?" I teased. "It's unisex," he said, smiling.

I left them to the headquarters improvements, and headed out to explore the tower. In full sun, Tallil's dirt, buildings and taxiways had no color except haze. But I made out the tall silhouette and kept walking.

I chided myself about Wurm along the way. Seriously. We both have jobs to do. I'm pretty sure "flirting" isn't one of them.

I was headed to the airfield's control tower. As the men and I had explored the base that morning, we'd run into a new Texas connection, Lt. Col. Greg Petrequin. He was an Air Force pilot with Texas roots. Petrequin had previously served as a KC-135 navigator out of Dyess Air Force Base in Abilene; he'd loved that aircraft and the job so much that he'd named his youngest daughter Kacie. When he heard about my own Dyess connections, he said I had to come visit the tower and meet his boss.

Tallil's air control tower was a piece of work that would have given OSHA a heart attack. The rusted metal stairs weren't really attached to the wall, or even to each other. The door was another slamming piece of metal that shut with a cloud of dust.

Air Force Col. A. Ray Myers met me at the top. Slight, athletic, grayed. He stared out of the dirty window at a line of incoming C-130s. The planes were a point of pride for a man who was here just six hours after the 3rd Infantry Division swept through. He arrived ready to get the still hostile and occupied runway operational for U.S. forces. He was also a kind and wizened grandfather on the assignment of a lifetime.

I had my head down taking notes, busy planning my next story. So it took a moment for Myers' offer to register.

"I'm headed to Baghdad. Want to come?"

I walked back to the guys and our emerging camp. Our cots and netting, boxes of bottled water and MREs were spread throughout the temporary sandy headquarters. These were the first tendrils of an eight-year mission in Iraq. It was a simple camp where everyone had their home — their cot. I lay quietly that night hearing the voices of Kolfage and Cortez talking trash, of Fuller and Washington setting up their security perimeter plans for this newly formed airbase. I thought about my choice: to stay with these men, who had kept me safe and were becoming so familiar. To see where their story went next. Or go to Baghdad.

It was the last time war was ever distant, when I made that choice. Even with the shots we heard at Camp Bucca and the occasional spiraling mushroom of smoke we saw from airstrikes at nearby Nasiriyah, despite the danger and lack of reliable sleep, food, water or a bathroom, war so far had felt … safe.

It was still the Iraq before Blackwater, and the Iraq before the massive U.S. contractor-run military cafeterias that popped up all over the country, serving wasteful amounts of glass-encased gelato hand scooped by third country nationals. I went to sleep after taking a sip of water from a dust-covered bottle, and eating a bit of the cement-paste MRE peanut butter, because it was the Iraq before country-western dance night and Wednesday's baked potato bar. I thought about my choice in the Iraq before ISIS and the terrifying deeply buried and vehicle-borne IEDs, and before the 107 mm round that hit Kolfage. It was a few days before I attended my first battlefield memorial service, and before the 4,505 that followed. On this night, Iraq was outdoor camping with a bucket for a shower, the hopefulness that what the young men did here would not only make history, but also help make

Iraq a better place. I woke to the raw, sharp holler of Cortez knifing a desert scorpion off his sleeping bag. And I knew I had to go.

3

So This Is War

aghdad, Iraq 2003
Baghdad. It streamed beneath us in yellow lines of blurred street lamps as our blacked-out U.S. Air Force C-130 threw itself across the city at an altitude of 500 feet.

Onboard it was completely dark, save for the green haze of the instrument panel. The pilots were flying by night vision goggles. The crew passed around a small glowstick when someone needed to read.

April 10, 2003. It was less than 24 hours since U.S. forces used an armored personnel carrier to drag down a statue of Saddam Hussein in downtown Baghdad. Swarms of cheering Iraqis climbed on the fallen stone, happily insulting his carved head with the bottom of their shoes. To Myers it was a signal: It was time to prepare the city's international airport for the swarms of gray tails and chartered humanitarian flights demanding to land there. But the airport still wasn't cleared of fighting. So these first C-130s flew with no exterior lights. They were just shadows that moved close and fast to the earth for extra protection.

For most of the flight I was in the cargo hold. Myers sat next to me. Around our bench, we were surrounded by the tools of war operations: netting filled to capacity with pallets of supplies and heavy equipment for runway repairs. Communications gear. Servers. Satellite dishes. Medical supplies. Water. Above our heads, the C-130's dim yellow auxiliary lighting cast a sickly hue on the colonel and me, and on the many wet lines of dirty sweat that dripped off my hairline and pooled under my body armor. "She's an old E model, so the AC's not as good," Myers kindly told me. "But she's a proud old bird. A veteran."

Myers was signaled back into the cockpit and motioned me to follow. We were close to landing. As he got up, he stretched and offered his best advice:

"The first 72 hours are always chaotic, disorienting. Sometimes you feel like you are really about to lose control, but the system is designed to let it all come together," he said. Then he headed up the stairs.

In the darkness, the crew was executing combat entry. The flight engineer purged the fuel masts while the pilot stepped on the rudder to drain any lingering gas. I strained to see out the cockpit windows, expecting to see war. But without night vision goggles, all I saw were black rolls of land and the occasional quiet outline of a box-shaped home. It felt like we were sailing, not flying, and I wanted to reach my hand out the window and run it along the dark swells of land below.

"I can see the runway!" I chirped to Myers, just as a shrill automated cockpit voice warned me quiet. "500!" "300!" "Minimum!" "Minimum!"

With a shaking jolt we rolled to a stop. As Myers warned, the first 72 hours wholly disoriented me.

The first 72 hours were 101st Airborne Military Police trucks that darted right up to our C-130 upon landing — much to the colonel's discomfort — and waved us with flashlights toward a looming, blacked-out building that was Baghdad's air control tower. I don't remember much about that first night. I know the night itself was not very long, only three hours, I thought as I pushed up from the filthy tower floor to stumble outside, groggy, into the morning sun. I brushed my teeth with a water bottle in the open air and spit toothpaste in the dirt.

In the daylight Myers could see the unacceptable. His runway and his taxiways were used as ramp space for Bradley Fighting Vehicles and short cuts for M1 Abrams tanks. So "Morning One" in Baghdad was administrative war; an immediate stare down involving Myers, the 101st Airborne Division and the 3rd Infantry Division.

In the daylight I also saw that Baghdad International Airport was a maze of expansive green-shaded arches and terminals that were mostly intact. There were rows of regular green and white Iraqi Airways 737s, luggage trucks and mobile jet ways. Everything an operating airport needed — even a gift shop of liquor that was untouched and now guarded. Everything except people. This does not look like war, I thought, except for the smoking remains of a few of the 737s caught in the firefight just three days before we landed.

"They tried to hold the airfield, but our Army's just too strong," our escort proudly told me.

"They're thinking, 'Gee, it's the Air Force, they just got here,'" one of our crew muttered under his breath. Myers pressed on.

"We've got to do something about these Army vehicles," Myers said. "They can't be on the flight line."

A few seconds later, an MP escorting us fell back and walked with me. "This colonel needs to meet our general," he warned. "Because there's probably going to be a dispute."

The meeting was colonel to colonel. Myers ended up in a face-to-face with Col. Jack Sterling, chief of staff to the 3rd Infantry Division.

"Do you see what you've got moving across here? Tanks," Sterling said. "They've got to move across somewhere. You've got to understand that."

"Your tanks just kicked up dirt on the taxiway our C-130 landed on last night," Myers returned. In the daylight I saw our sharp jolt and short landing wasn't due to a threat; it was because we couldn't use the runway. It had several 75-foot wide holes in it from U.S. bombs.

"We need a sterile environment here, this is definitely not an environment for aircraft. Develop a route around the airfield until the runway is repaired," Myers requested.

"The runway," Sterling sniffed, "has three large craters in it courtesy of the Air Force."

The conversation and its secondary goals seemed at an impasse. Myers wanted airfield control to be centrally located, but the spot he wanted was already in use. It was bedding down rows of 101st Apache and Black Hawk helicopters. Myers reminded his Army colleague of the hundreds of tons of cargo and aid inbound on airlifters requesting clearance to land; there was no time for this.

His colleague reminded him that they, the Army, also welcomed the aid.

"We need that," Sterling said. "We've been fighting for 21 days." The impasse softened. Sterling would clear the tanks; Myers would have his runway. The Army would get supplied.

We walked out back into the sunlight and I noticed the colonel had a little more spring in his step.

"I need to do a quick tour to ensure the strip is ready," Myers said. "And then get back to send some emails that say, 'release the hounds.'"

In the first 72 hours before I even got outside the wire, war came in. It came to a massive hangar filled with an unearthly haze of white sunlight as a young man began to speak.

"This isn't how we planned!" Army Spc. Chad Wofford choked as he talked about his lost best friend, 26-year-old Sgt. Mike Pedersen. "It was just the other day we were talkin' about what it was going to be like when we got out of here."

Inside the hangar, two Black Hawk helicopters pointed center, a memorial watch over their perished crew. In a nighttime crash in Karbala six men of the Black Hawk "Storm 6" perished: a newlywed; a West Pointer; a future Harvard grad; an air mission commander. It left their sister crew, another six men who stood before all assembled, brokenhearted.

Six battle crosses faced the crowd. They were made of empty

helmets, dog tags and combat boots; each hung on wooden racks that cast long shadows on the hangar floor. The daylight poured in from the half-closed hangar doors and filled the vast space as rows 20 deep of the battalion's five companies sang the first verses of tribute to their ultimate sacrifice:

"You who dwell in the shelter of the Lord," their welling voices cracked, "who abide in his shadow for life "

"He was the best man at my wedding, and the only man that I not only approved of, but gave my blessing to date my little sister," Spc. Joseph Arteno said, weeping about his lost other half,

22-year-old Spc. Matt Boule.

A respectful line of soldiers filed past the hanging helmets. "You never prepared me for this!" Wofford cried out. "I want

you to know a person like you comes around only once in a lifetime. And that I love you. We all love you. So keep your head up, 'cause I'll see you when I get there."

I was supposed to be an observer. But their words constricted around my heart faster than I could fight them down through my pen. I tightened my grip around the brown suede notebook that held every thought and tried to do my job. But when the ceremony ended, the mourners remained. I would see them on the air base's footpaths and in its tents. When I was back at the encampment that Myers had allowed me to use, I was surrounded by the small group of now-familiar crew who ate and slept there. The white glow of my computer under Baghdad's open sky was not a screen of privacy but an invitation for troops to talk. There was no distance and I quickly lost track of the distinction between work and war.

Then I got outside the wire. And war was waiting there too.

Like much that happened in Iraq, each new experience was based on a chance meeting. A day into our arrival at Baghdad,

I met 422nd Civil Affairs Battalion Maj. Linda Scharf. When I overheard that she and her team were headed downtown for a humanitarian mission, I asked to come along. I needed to see this city beyond the TV scenes I'd watched on CNN.

Baghdad up close was a ghost town. I saw street after street of six-and eight-story white or tan cement buildings, some with balconies draped with drying rugs. But not a soul in sight.

We pulled up to the Red Crescent hospital, where team members escorted a pair of U.S. Agency for International Development doctors inside to check the hospital's dwindling medical supplies.

Scharf and the drivers did not enter, she stayed outside with me. We lingered on the road by a detachment of Marines who'd been assigned to protect the hospital.

Scharf was an Army reservist who in real life specialized in oil and natural gas manufacturing. She was part of a Civil Affairs battalion, an army of experts in civic functions like health care, law, electricity and plumbing who come in with the main wave of forces to help stabilize a city after the fighting stops.

When she deployed to Iraq she assumed would be assigned to help get its oil infrastructure working again. Instead she was told to build Iraq's schools. But she'd been pulled from that assignment too and that day was instructed to escort doctors into Baghdad. She drove the last Humvee in our convoy. Her vehicle was completely open. The soldiers had removed its canvas top and the Humvee's doors so they would be able to shoot, if necessary, in all directions. The oil expert turned-schools-expert-turned-chauffeur was going to make her first ride into Baghdad in an open air convertible.

Outside the Red Crescent it was bright, hot, uncomfortable.

Scharf and I made small talk with one of the Marines assigned to guard the street. While we chatted, they made lunch. One cursed as steam burst out of his MRE cook bag, burning his raw and blistered hands.

Gunfire broke the silence. The shots sounded too far away to be a threat, but I backed up a bit toward the Marines anyway.

A dirty white Mercedes screamed around the corner and drove full speed toward our position.

"Watch out, it could be a suicide bomber!" The men dropped their meals and raised their weapons.

I don't know if I froze. I know I didn't jump into the Humvee. I think I jumped behind it. You don't really know what you do in those moments, until your mind unfreezes and you get a second to figure out where you planted your feet.

It wasn't a suicide bomber. The driver was civilian, wailing in anguished screams. He pushed out of his car door with his hands in the air and begged for help. Beside him was a young woman. When he opened the passenger door to bring her inside the hospital, her body slumped toward the pavement into a pool of blood. Her feet dragged and scraped the ground. The back of her head was open, her remaining long brown hair clumped in streaks of dark red.

I was about eight feet away.

I did not smell her blood. Maybe death only smells when it has time to sink in. I was busy calculating a choice:

Do I go help, or be silent and observe?

She was dead, she was dead, she was dead. Was she dead? The Marines did not move. Neither did I. I exhaled when Red Crescent hospital doctors grabbed the man, taking him and the bleeding girl inside.

We all have jobs to do. But shouldn't I be doing more? Who the hell was I not to?

"I don't think she was alive," Scharf said as the doctors took her in. "Another innocent pays the price."

The Marine went back to eating his spaghetti.

***

Before our trip outside the wire had started that day, as the handful of Humvees that would make this mission queued up, Scharf talked to me about the Army at large; how even in Baghdad, war was a remote concept.

"You know only seven percent of the military has ever seen combat, right?" she said.

I nodded. It was a pretty well-known statistic, one that the media regurgitated in the days leading up to "shock and awe."

Then on our return trip from the hospital, as we drove back down Palestine Street through that empty, haunted downtown, we came under fire.

"Get ready!" Scharf's lieutenant colonel bristled. Her front-seat passenger was looking ahead to two men on the sidewalk. He did not like what he saw and grabbed for the radio.

"They are wearing military boots under the robes!" The radioed warning blared into my Humvee — I wasn't riding with Scharf. She'd wanted me in a hardened vehicle, one that had a roof and a turret for shooting back.

The first vehicle to pass waved to the robed men on the street. They did not wave back.

"Get down! Get down!" our Humvee lead yelled at me. He started directing our crew. "Wait until you see where it's coming from!"

I jerked up instead of down and looked up and out. What nondescript building was shooting at us? Was it from the street? "Get down!" he shouted again and I crouched over my knees and pushed my helmet into my shoulder blades.

"Keep your weapon ready!" he yelled at his crew. "Watch your rear! As soon as you see a muzzle flash, light it up!"

Bullets are ethereal things when you are in a Humvee that is driving through them. The actual firing is distant; when the bullets hit, they ping like rocks. I turned my neck, trying to see ... anything. All I could see was green Army metal and a dirty window.

The pings that were loud and fast were bullets on us. Then there were the muffled engines and shots as the Humvees to our front and rear faced more fire.

A few Humvees behind us, Scharf was in a focused blur. Just watch the bumper ahead of you. She could hear the bullets on her vehicle and winced as they ricocheted off her windshield and hood. Her ears were ringing and she couldn't understand the passenger beside her. She gripped the wheel and pushed her vehicle even closer to the Humvee in front of her. Drive faster! When all vehicles had cleared the first kill zone, she could not believe what she heard next.

"We're going too far! We're in the Red Zone!" the lead Humvee radioed to the line. "Pull over!"

The Red Zone was how the military marked neighborhoods that were still fighting, and our humanitarian escort was not set for that kind of fight. The Humvees quickly pulled off the street to assess what needed to happen.

The lead vehicle suggested more blind turns.

You assholes, Scharf thought. *You've gotten us lost.*

All the vehicles moved again, to one U-turn followed by another to try to return to another known route. We drove instead into kill zone two.

"Up on the left! Up on the left! Start shooting!" our driver shouted to the turret gunner standing beside me. All I could see

31

were his legs.

Shoot where? The Humvees were surrounded and gunfire exploded around the Humvee in front of us from a balcony or maybe a roof. The vehicles sped and swerved, and as they did I saw white tracers from AK-47 fire streak down.

We were racing past 3rd Infantry Division personnel carriers; the soldiers there were crouched and pinned against their vehicles. Scharf saw them in the periphery as we drove past.

Get up! Shoot back! Protect us! Her mind screamed.

I was on autopilot, writing as fast as my scared hand would work. The pages of my notebook filled with massive scrawl, incomplete thoughts and the words of each crew member.

"My weapon's jammed!" our gunner yelled as we raced through two city blocks. Our convoy entered a third volley of gunfire. "Where's it coming from?" he yelled again. "Take the SAW!!"

The soldier reached down from the turret and grabbed for the heavy mounted gun. The vehicles roared through. We cleared the third round of attack and the gunfire dissipated. We went from absolute violence to total quiet. There was not a sound save our engines powering us back toward the Green Zone.

Once we were back in the safety of base, the troops walked up and down the line and assessed the bullet holes in the vehicles. Remarkably, everyone had come home uninjured. The worst off was Scharf and her Humvee.

The bullet holes were in the glass by her face, and in the Humvee bar behind her head. But they had missed her. There was a moment of silent contemplation for everyone.

Scharf had a fellow soldier take a photo of her sitting in her driver's seat, with the bullet holes beside her head. It was evidence of how close she came to dying that day.

No one is going to believe me when I tell them, she thought.

I knew I had a story to write. I wanted my editors to know. But I didn't really want to leave; neither did anyone else in the crew. When word got out, more onlookers arrived, wanting to see evidence of the hostility that waited outside the wire.

As the crowd dwindled, Scharf completed her mission debrief with the drivers and turned toward her tent. On her way out she grabbed my shoulder.

"Pretty eventful, huh?" she held me in her gaze as she passed. "Welcome to the seven percent."

Scharf made sure I was OK. Then she went to the refuge of her cot inside the airport's passenger waiting area. She was shaking badly and did not want me or her fellow soldiers to see.

Since the morning began she'd had doubts about the wisdom of this mission. She'd lost faith in the commander leading the convoy that day. His bad decisions had pushed them into three kill zones. She was viciously angry at the faceless Iraqis who were shooting at her. She was here to help!

Scharf got back to her cot and took out a pad of paper and let go. She wrote pages and pages filled with anger and resentment and fear. She wrote and wrote until she thought it was out of her system, because she had never experienced this level of hatred and she was terrified.

***

In May 2003 I returned from Iraq and re-entered my Washing-ton life. I was still with my D.C. boyfriend, trying to reconcile home with what I'd experienced overseas. Whole Foods made me overwhelmed. Delivery sushi made me guilt-ridden. I ordered it anyway.

I had no sense of what was real. Was it war? Was it the desert?

Was it this life in Washington, with its weekends at Home Depot and weeknights in front of the TV? Was this "embed" just a short-lived journalistic test in a make-believe world of bright desert sun that had real Iraqi suffering and real dead soldiers in a situation that was so desperately unfair for so many, but for me had become this door-opening adventure?

And there was more: I'd cheated.

I'd become that stupid "Three Kings" cliché.

I panicked. If I didn't quickly veer away and force my way back onto D.C.'s path of stability, I'd lose whatever foundation was left.

I took a drag of my cigarette, ordered another beer and looked across the bar.

It was a Friday night in Washington, D.C. I was out by myself, writing thoughts in my journal as I tried to put sense to feeling:

Late night in a downtown Washington bar, a pretty blonde squeezed past to the bathroom, her hair and steps backlit by hazy bar lights. Her date was boyish and handsome. He brushed his finger down their sweating beer glasses as he waited, tracing wet circles into the wood.

When she returned, he leaned into her forehead.

I was a few chairs away, judging them from a beer-blurred distance at a cigarette-strewn booth. Without a word, I heard her. She didn't freefall for this one. But she didn't hurt, either. She didn't push too hard, and he was content to stay.

It became another American marriage.

I sat in the bar booth and lit a Marlboro. *I'll be different. Can't you see?* Look in my eyes. Tell me you see my hope. And I'll fall in love with you before you finish this sentence.

***

In my mind, I was back in Tallil on my last night with the Goodfellow crew. All around us the airstrip was open for business — more than 1,000 military personnel had spilled onto the base since we'd first arrived. Which meant the crew's escort detail was complete. That next day we would part: Wurm, Cortez, Kolfage and Holmes would return to Kuwait, to Al Jaber Air Base. I would board a C-130 for Baghdad.

The guys built a campfire and Kolfage shared the rest of his tobacco stash. In the darkness we could hear the engines of nearby Black Hawks preparing for flight, and the ever-present and welcome smell of jet fuel that lingered on the sandy air.

In the firelight I saw a bond reflected in their faces. They knew their first war story was coming to an end.

"You're all welcome for the cigars," Kolfage sassed. "Thannnks, Kolfage," they responded.

I passed around my brown suede diary and asked each of them to write what they felt.

"So others may live," Cortez wrote, citing Air Force pararescue. "Only quote that explains why I'm here."

"This whole experience made me have a totally different outlook on life," Kolfage wrote. "It's hard to appreciate what you have until you go to a third world country."

"I hope to come back in five years and see a permanent Air Force base, keeping the peace," Holmes wrote. "Then I can say I was part of the first few."

And then there was Wurm.

"So there I was, sitting around a campfire in *expletive* Iraq, hoping Timmy Jihad wasn't sneaking in after us. Looking back years from now I will know we did something good for these people. Right now there's not time to stop and feed the hungry, but soon relief will start to flow, and people in this part of the world will know we aren't as bad as they think."

Wurm: 28 like me, but already graying. A highly quotable, smartass Texan, my heart didn't stand a chance.

That last night together, as the guys gathered, I realized too late I needed to get military clearance to fly. It was already dark; there was no desk phone, of course. So it was either walk or hitch a ride to ask the air control tower in person.

"I'll take you," Wurm said. We headed for a dusty ATV the guys used to move around the airfield.

I climbed on the back and clung on to his body armor. Under the night sky, we raced past shelled buildings and tree silhouettes. This close and this dark, each blurred, blacked-out tank and personnel carrier we passed looked like accidental death.

But all I could hear in my head was Nick Drake's "Northern Sky."

"Let's take the long way back," I told him after I received clearance.

"I wanted to grab your hand, but I was afraid you'd slap me," he said.

"I wanted you to kiss me," I said back.

But then I'd parted from him; I'd gone to Baghdad without Wurm and the guys. War went from safe and distant to raw and unrelentingly close. I'd witnessed a battlefield funeral and shared in the seven percent. And at night under the white glow of my computer screen, as I spent those weeks by Baghdad's control tower, I'd stare each night at the inbox, hoping there was an email.

And not from my soon-to-be ex-boyfriend back home.

It seemed once I was surrounded by men who had far less, and gave far more, I forgot to miss him.

"Never been this confined before," Wurm wrote me. After the open canvas of Iraq, Kuwait's Al Jaber Air Base was hard to return to. And sometimes he signed, "xox."

"At a crossroads," I wrote in my journal. "Maybe after some harder living in Baghdad, maybe then will I come back to D.C., to my boyfriend and our friends in Washington and realize this calm and constant life is good?"

It didn't happen that way. It never does.

Instead, once I got back to Al Jaber, I looked for Wurm. I found him in that maze of Kuwaiti air base buildings and asked if he had time to get together. When he walked into my temporary dorm, every sense – the anticipation, the awkwardness, the not knowing what was the right thing to say – it was all back where it was in those first stifling hours in the Humvee. We spent about two hours in hopeless small talk. We traced the lines of each other's hands. And then we were naked and jawing away on a roll-away spring mattress stained with the corpses of dozens of brown bedbugs.

But I knew even before he touched me that there was something missing.

Truth, the moment after Wurm went from a wartime ideal to daylight infidelity, Nick Drake's "Northern Sky" started to die a little more.

This wasn't right, either. It just … wasn't. I couldn't understand why. But the last few days on base, as I packed up my things and wandered around to say goodbye to the men and women I'd covered, we avoided each other.

I returned to D.C., rootless. I didn't want to leave Iraq, I even begged my editors to stay. This wasn't how the story was supposed to end. But as I walked around base, with its temporary buildings that provided laundry, a computer café and coffee, I saw the young men and women in uniform there. They were talking with each other, laughing and bonding over a single purpose.

Their job was to stay, to do what their country asked. I could leave or do whatever I wished.

The embed program had made me feel a part of it. The instant

I left that bubble the military's temporary membership had been yanked back with a quick reminder: I was an outsider.

And I needed to get back to acting like one.

So I boarded a flight for home. But I didn't belong back in Washington, either. The accolades for reporting were appreciated but discomforting. I had the prize I'd envied about my fellow correspondents at the Hilton. I had my own war story now.

But I didn't understand it. I had not expected opportunity or a sense of aliveness or a sense of belonging and I lost balance making room for this new world in the conflicted emotions that this war was also a place where I'd already seen terrible loss and I knew there would be more.

Those desert sensations of aliveness began to fade almost as soon as I got back. It didn't seem to matter whether I spent some of my reporting bonus on new shoes or gave that money to charity; whether I drank with friends until I got emotional or ended up telling off an unfortunately timed query, "I was not going to talk about Iraq." I was uneven and unfair and not unlike a 4-year-old who had just heard a new curse word, and was now testing the boundaries of this expanded verbal world.

If I did nothing, would war just become a new line on my résumé? From there, move on?

If I went back and stayed, would it be any different? I stayed home, but I was treading water.

On those days after returning, sometimes it was Sunday afternoon and I'd just half-heartedly slept with my D.C. boyfriend. Twelve hours later it was Monday, and I was back to covering Congress.

Sometimes it was a Friday night, and I was alone in a bar booth imagining everything the blonde would regret about her compromise.

So many nights, I was naked in bed, trying not to hurt a good man.

And every moment, I was not there.

4

The Unfinished Stack

C*arlsbad, CA., 2003*
    Three weeks after I came home from Iraq I was in my grandmother's kitchen, watching her slice raw chicken on a worn plastic board. Her hands were still elegant for their 78 years, her nails manicured and painted red. She set the meat,

firmed the blade, and pushed.

"You know, your grandfather wrote about the war, too," she said.

I had always called her Abuela, which is Spanish for "grandmother." Abuela was a Chilean beauty, the room's top prize the night my grandfather met her while on assignment in Latin America, two years after World War II. Age never dimmed her expressive eyes, nor thinned her thick eyebrows, nor faded the deep dimples that softened the elegant stature of her high forehead and cheekbones.

Abuela's words pulled me back into the present. *She shouldn't be doing all the cooking alone.* I reached for cooking sherry from the shelf and handed her a cube of bouillon. Polite movements I hoped were helpful enough. Then my mind wandered again.

I'd been tossed out of my now ex-boyfriend's house and nothing about my life fit anymore. So I went to the safest place I knew. Abuela's Carlsbad, Calif., home.

I came for the calming effect of her rooms, which were always off-white with one wall of accent color. I came for the cool California mornings that started when sunlight burst past the lemon tree outside her bedroom window and gently woke her to begin a session of yoga. I came for Abuela's company on walks through Carlsbad's mist-covered hills, followed by laps in her community's steaming outdoor pool. My grandmother had a tranquility that fed an intimate calmness. In her bathroom, where a black and white swimsuit hung clean and her counter held only perfume and a jar of face cream, you walked in and felt everything was in its place, each inanimate object obliging with its own stillness, a presence. Like her.

Anytime my life seemed out of control I came, and she helped restore order to the chaos. So after Iraq, I came.

Once we'd finished eating, Abuela walked toward her living room.

"Ay darling, help me open this."

We stopped at a heavy African wood chest Abuela kept between two cream-colored leather couches. We moved her artwork and family photographs and lifted the lid.

Inside the chest there were rows and rows of navy and brown fake leather photo albums, their gummed yellow sheets stained with age. The early pages started with photos of my grandfather and his younger brother Terry as kids in California. Photos of the boys camping in a tent on their front lawn. Others of them fishing, then sparring with epee swords. Then pages of the brothers as young men in uniform, Terry 23, my grandfather 25. Terry, or Staff Sgt. Terrence "Salty" Harris as he was known by Easy Company, 101st Airborne. Terry was already a World War II legend due to Steven Ambrose and HBO's "Band of Brothers." He was always the one willing to jump first into fist fights with his calculating and swift older brother beside him. In one of the last photos we had of him, Terry stood in an open field in England with his arms around his fellow paratroopers. It was taken just before D-Day and his jump onto the blood fields of Normandy.

After that my grandfather was in the war pages alone. There was the photo of his bomber. Another, this time a close up of the aircraft's riveted sides, shot up with bullet holes. Then a photo of my grandfather on base during the war, his back perfectly straight even as he leaned over a desk, staring at paperwork. "Richard C. Harris, Commanding Officer," the desk plate read.

Then a last portrait of him in dress whites, distinguished, chest back, gold braid and medals set, when there was no more shooting left to do.

When enough albums were lifted out and scattered on the floor, new stacks of paper came into view. They had been pushed into the corner of her storage chest and left untouched. The pages were slightly gritty from years of dust. Even the paperclips were perfectly aligned.

My grandfather's memoirs.

How long have these been here? I wondered.

"Oh, I typed all of these!" Abuela said, eyeballing text she hadn't seen since he'd passed away.

"Dick would talk and talk, and then he would say, 'No! No! Go back!' When he thought something wasn't remembered correctly. Oh we had such a time of it."

U.S. Air Force Col. Richard Conant Harris was a lion of a man who'd lived terrified he'd wake up one day sentenced to a conventional life. In my mind, my grandfather was this warrior, forever feathering the propellers of his heavy bomber as he raced fuel and time back to base after another terrible mission. After the war, he was the charming U.S. Air Force attaché who thrived in the heady politics of post-war Latin America and Europe. He whisked a 23-year-old Abuela away from her mother in Chile and into a lifetime in the headlines; postings in Spain, Argentina and Mexico as the U.S. injected new military bases and influence around the globe to ensure that America would never again fight another world war.

But he was also Col. Richard Conant Harris, USAF (ret.), who died March 20, 1989. Official cause of death: cardiac arrest. In those final years, my grandfather knew he was dying. Sheets full of VA clinic paperwork spelled out the ailments: plaque in the arteries; a persistent nervous condition; diabetes; a deteriorating spine; gastrointestinal distress. And a "long history of left precordial and left arm pain" — honor injuries among all

Liberator pilots who gripped the heavy bomber with their left arm and fought the plane's yoke for 8, 10, 12 hours a mission.

In those final months his liver was failing. His hands shook. His skin yellowed. On good days he left notes around the house, instructions about whom Abuela was to call when he died; how she was to adjust Veterans Affairs benefits so she would be cared for throughout the rest of her life.

On bad days, Abuela wrote pages and pages of her own about the mental anguish the VA missed. In their Carlsbad home, right about his third drink in, my grandfather would scream and threaten her. He'd cry and fall into a memory from 30 years before. My grandmother no longer counted how many times in their marriage she dried him out, made excuses to his office, hid him at home. He thanked her like a child. But as soon as he regained strength, he'd pour another cocktail and live out the last of his glory days – threatening to throw her out of the house if she touched his glass. She no longer fought him. He'd pour a scotch in the late morning and command her to type, and they would continue on like this through the afternoon, until he passed out or lost his mind. If he passed out, it was a good day. "In the end, when his brain had completely deteriorated, he started to be abusive in bad language, telling me he did not want me anymore, that he wanted a young woman, a young body, and threw me out of the house," my grandmother confided.

His madness swung almost immediately, every time. "Then he would send me flowers to the motel I was staying at," Abuela said.

After dinner, when the dishes were done and Abuela had gone to bed, I curled up with a glass of wine and the stack of pages of my grandfather's text.

He died when I was 15, before I was old enough to appreciate he had a story to tell. My parents had separated long before. My grandfather became a person I knew only through phone calls and photographs as our one family became two. I'd needed my grandfather then, and I needed him now. In the years of absence I'd built him into the memory I wanted him to be: forever the war hero in my mind. As I reported in Iraq that spring, that distanced, romanticized belief of how war heroes are and how war stories go went to Iraq with me.

The desert had different plans. War was not what I'd expected it to be and I was not ready for the ways war came home with me.

So when I held my grandfather's dusty pages they felt like treasure. I scanned each chapter, excited. I read the lines, looking for a way to reframe my own experience.

But his text did not have the war I expected either.

Instead, page by page my heart sank a little more. What I found was frustratingly unfinished text. No names of bases, squadrons, exact missions or dates. No obvious war hero story. I saw lines where he went over the typed words with a pen to insert, revise. His handwritten edits betrayed so many thoughts that were lost to his incoherence even as his mind fought to get them on the page.

Worse, I couldn't turn a page without reading about another English, Canadian or Italian girl he slept with. Like his airborne conquests, his sexual ones didn't name names either.

The sense of shame and unsteadiness I'd felt in coming home from Iraq returned with a heated blush. There was no redemption here.

This isn't my grandfather, I thought.

This isn't the man posed proudly in dress whites, a Distinguished Flying Cross and Purple Heart on his chest.

Were the facts lost because your mind had already gone? I asked him. *There's more to this,* I said.

I'll tell your story the way it should have been told. You were just sick. You weren't able to remember.

A light flickered, an idea began to hold.

As I drifted to sleep a new plan took shape. I'd finish my grandfather's war story. For both of us.

***

The next day, Abuela and I got dressed with an errand in store — to make a Kinko's copy of my grandfather's memoir text for me. Abuela also wanted to shop for a few things and pick up her medicines, which meant we were headed to the on-base exchange at Marine Corps Base Camp Pendleton. For Abuela this was an outing to dress for. She put on a light gray vest and clipped on two silver earrings. She pulled one of her favorite silver cross pendants from her bureau and slipped it over her neck. She ran her hands down her body, a motion that ensured the smoothness of the outfit. Her entrance was polished with a touch of red lipstick and a spritz of Sanborns' Orange Blossom; an easy elegance.

Decades after their deaths both my grandfather and Abuela's mother, Yolanda, made sure we knew they were still around.

We drove to Camp Pendleton's main gate and slowed for inspection. Marines spotted my grandfather's old colonel sticker in the windshield and stiffened to salute. It gave me chills. Abuela gave them a happy wave.

"I just love when they do that," she beamed as we drove through. "It's Daddy, you know, saying hello."

Once we were inside the base's exchange, with its rows of generic brand clothing and inexpensive watches, Abuela detoured to the perfume, where her mother waited.

Abuela scanned the perfume counter for Chanel No. 5, and dabbed the sample to her neck. She closed her eyes as Yolanda and a sea of memories drifted around their Chilean daughter in an embrace.

"It was her favorite," Abuela said. "It is mine too."

The Wound-up Punch

Freshman-Sophmore Brawl
Glendale College - 1935

lendale, CA., 1935

G   In life few things bound my grandfather to earth. So it was understandable that in death he barely tolerated entrapment in my fraying Kinko's box.

Inside the box it was 1935: Richard "Dick" Harris was youth and muscle and salt caked in mud and a smile as he and younger brother Terry egged on yet another fight. It was 1940; he was bursting through the sleeves of his slate blue U.S. Army Air Corps

Cadet uniform and teetering at the edge of a runway and war. It was 1944; he was fighting a dying bomber hit by enemy fire, determined to get back to base. It was Dec. 3, 1947; he was standing in the doorway of a U.S. Embassy-Argentina cocktail party, looking up the lines of a black off-the-shoulder Christian Dior "New Look" dress and into the deep hazel eyes of Abuela.

It was all of these things at once and none of them, for it was actually the final months of his life and Dick sat for hours in a white leather recliner, dictating his memoirs as Abuela typed. He leaned back in a cotton guayabera and wore eyeglasses that darkened in the sun. He drank scotch at 11 a.m. and his cigarette smoke was curling, curling.

The early paragraphs of my grandfather's memoirs were as clear as the California days he spent living them. His was a childhood of sport, hunting and fishing, and by 17 my grandfather was in his physical prime, darkly tanned and shirtless with washboard abs from years of outdoorsmanship.

But he was no saint. Dick's hair was invariably glittered with sweat; his sharp gray eyes with pranks and trouble. On this day, like so many others, he stood over his latest victim, another high school boy who'd dared take on little brother Terry's taunting, as Terry paced behind, ready to swing again.

"Harris!"

Both boys turned to see the Dean of Men at Glendale High School striding in long angry steps toward them. Bill Sawyer, Dick's best friend and always his second when they started these melees, grabbed their dusty cotton button-down shirts from the school yard and tossed them up into each boys' hands.

"My office, now!"

The elder Dick Harris, the boys' father, had picked Glendale, California, to raise his family in the early 1920s as he and millions of other men were shed from the Army's ranks following World War I. He adored the little community and the neat, enviable life it could provide, often found in the pages under "perfect." Glendale was in a canyon, surrounded by streams and horse trails from the nearby Verdugo Hills. Glendale was just east of nascent Hollywood, a proud community that boasted it was a "city of good moral influences," ruled by church and club. The homes that dotted Glendale were English or Spanish in style, their trim front lawns just as likely to be graced by tall pines as they were swaying palms.

In this peaceful, structured home the elder Harris taught his young sons to fish and hunt and defend their little sister Annette. He directed both sons to the local 1,000-strong Glendale Boy Scouts chapter while he began his climb on the community boards, the Oakmont Country Club and Glendale's 2,500 member Elks Club.

They were boys raised with their father's strict principles of faith, honor, self-discipline and perfectionism. He had specific plans for the lives of each of his sons. Terry would earn a commission to the U.S. Naval Academy; Dick, to West Point.

But by the time Dick was 17 and Terry was 15, both boys were derailing their father's dreams for them. Glendale's main street, its Owl Drug Store, the daylight gossip of Glendale High and even its main attraction, The Alexander Theatre – where movies from next-door Hollywood often debuted – was a world too small. Suffocating. In their high school senior years there would be no West Point commission for my grandfather, and no Annapolis invitation for Terry. They'd be lucky instead to barely graduate. The boys were quickly cutting off any options they had to leave.

Not that Dick didn't try. In 1936 he joined the Marine Corps Reserve, joining its drill team and earning medals in rifle and pistol target shooting. But medals were not what he'd joined the reserves for. Instead he put on his full dress uniform and walked into town to knock on the managing editor's door at the city's only newspaper, The Glendale News-Press. The editor was intrigued by the young man's uniformed presence and decided to listen to his earnest request.

"If you'll fund my trip to China, I'll join the Chinese Army and send back first-hand reports on the Sino-Japanese War," he said. Dick expected this answer would be yes. Why wouldn't it be? It was a cheap and valuable way for Glendale to learn what was happening. It could be important. It could mean world war. Glendale needed to know.

And I need to get out of Glendale, Dick thought.

The managing editor didn't want to laugh out loud and make this young man feel bad. Instead he thanked him for his good idea but told him it was not something the newspaper would be able to support. The next day the managing editor penned an Op-Ed: "The impossibility of covering a war from the vantage point of one soldier."

"All of Glendale shook their heads about 'that Harris kid,'" my grandfather wrote. "Especially the parents and fathers of my girlfriends."

Instead he enrolled in Glendale Junior College and found purpose in defending the honor of any damsel-in-distress whether the slight was real or conveniently imagined. He tried to do well by the rules of his father's house. But life at home too was unraveling by that point. Their mother, Myrtle Sheehan Harris, fell into a deep, bipolar illness. Terry did not get an Annapolis commission. My grandfather got thrown out of Glendale Junior College after one-too-many fights.

The elder Dick Harris had lost grip on his perfect home. He

moved Myrtle to the attic, ordering the children not to talk to her or see her, except to deliver her meals. At night, they could hear her screams. She died in 1937 during an uncomplicated surgery to relieve hypertension in her back; she was only 44.

All my grandfather wrote in his memoirs was, "I didn't cry."

The elder Harris worked to get both sons back on track. Upon graduation Terry enlisted in the Navy and enrolled in the Naval Academy Prep School in Rhode Island. The prep school was a second chance at a commission; this time he got it.

And then Terry threw that away, too.

Terry was just months away from graduation at Annapolis. He would be a commissioned Naval officer, just as his father dreamed.

But a few weeks before graduation he and four other midshipmen decided to go "over the wall" and sneak out to Washington, D.C., for a night out with the girls. They went AWOL.

It was 2 a.m. on the highway back to the academy when the driver fell asleep. Their car skidded across the highway and rolled on its back. All five midshipmen, Terry too, were taken by ambulance to the nearest hospital with serious injuries.

When they healed with just a handful of weeks to go before their anticipated commissioning, each was slapped with enough demerits that if they got one more, they would be "found," my grandfather wrote, "dismissed from the Academy."

"None of the five made it to graduation."

Bill Sawyer and Dick had planned to go to West Point together. Sawyer had made his West Point commission; Dick had not. So it was just my grandfather in Glendale now. He was restless. He took hard to liquor. He lost himself to the backseat of his girlfriend's car. But in a telling moment of father's influence, at the last minute Dick told his girlfriend he couldn't sleep with her.

He wrote about that too, remembering the words his father had said: *If you expect your wife to be a virgin, you should be one too.*

He'd become a wound-up punch, waiting to land.

In a last act the elder Harris arranged a job for his son in the city's newest six-story building, the Glendale Security & Trust. But to my grandfather, a stately brick office tower was not an opportunity. It was a cage.

I will not be stuck in my father's ranch house. I will not be the son who never escapes Glendale, he thought.

In his dreams, Dick was not left to a life in Glendale. He was a fighter pilot. It was an obsessive dream he fed through the newsreels at The Alexander as its films showed the buildup to war, squadrons of British warplanes lining up for the defense of Europe. In his daydreams he spun through fire and flack, shooting and diving fast to the deck where he died heroically. He became obsessed with the details of his dream, each night adding more risk, more edge.

One night he awoke with a plan. He knew how to leave this town and fight the war he was destined to fly for. He wanted to serve his nation. That was what heroes did.

He also wanted a ticket out of town.

Dick tested his way into pilot school, and in early 1940 he put on a new uniform: the slate blue blouse and trousers of a U.S. Army Air Corps Flying Cadet.

But it was still no escape. U.S. Army Air Cadet Richard Conant Harris was assigned to primary flight school with Class 40-H.

The school was located at Grand Central Air Terminal. In Glendale, California.

6

The Five Dollar Bet

S *an Diego, CA., 1941*

California's midwinter sun yawned into a lazy, pink dusk at the exclusive Hotel Del Coronado. Outside, wealthy families strolled from beachside games of tennis to the open bar, sipping cocktails as they toasted another Pacific sunset.

A few floors above them, in an oceanview room above the promenade, Ford Motor Company chief of production Charles

Sorenson did not notice these things. He was sketching with irritation on hotel stationery. The company man hadn't even bothered to change out of his business suit.

Sorenson's creative flow was more engineer than artist; each idea jotted down on a piece of paper and stacked in exacting piles on his small hotel desk. As the moon rose, his perfect stacks of ideas covered the carpet and the bed. He looked up intensely for a short break, then nosed down into his work once more.

Earlier in the day Sorenson had toured the factory floors of Consolidated Aircraft in San Diego. There on a football-field sized assembly room, Consolidated's president, Reuben Fleet, had proudly walked his corporate rival through every aspect of Consolidated's new bomber, the B-24.

The bomber was about the length of an extended city bus, with heavy, fuel-filled wings. It was too cumbersome for the Doolittle raid, too ugly to win over hearts as "The Flying Fortress." Consolidated's B-24 was single-purposed: to destroy. Every curve of the aircraft was designed to serve that cause, from the bomber's .50 caliber machine guns, its four tons of bombs and the fuel and reach to penetrate deep into the Axis.

With pride for his production, Fleet wrote to the Navy: "Here is a ship that would liberate the world from tyranny." Already the first models were shipped to Britain to hunt for German submarines. And somewhere between San Diego and London, Consolidated's flying weapon got its name: the Liberator.

Earlier that day Ford and Consolidated Aircraft had met at the request of President Franklin Delano Roosevelt. The nation only had a fledgling flight school system and a paltry air arsenal, and Roosevelt was anxious. He saw war on the horizon. He wanted these firms to work together.

It is the only way, Roosevelt said.

So Fleet opened his factory floor to Sorenson, and watched uncomfortably as his rival studied Consolidated's production line. Sorenson walked slowly, scowled occasionally. He took detailed, critical notes.

Share parts, assembly, ideas, Roosevelt said.

Sorenson could see his rival's eyes proudly catalog every aspect of the Liberator's fuselage as each bird moved diagonally down the line. *Every seam, every part assembled to perfection,* Fleet boasted. Thousands of painstaking man hours.

Sorenson viewed Fleet's approach differently. He was unimpressed by what he saw as inefficiency in Consolidated's production. Each bomber was built individually, with parts specific to the curves and idiosyncrasies of that particular aircraft.

This will never win a war, Sorenson thought, and said as much to Fleet. Consolidated and Ford both stiffened their posture.

"Well how would you do it then?" Fleet challenged.

"I'll have something in the morning," Sorenson returned, and started to build a bomber in his mind.

Throughout the night, as the ocean pushed and pulled outside his window, Sorenson thought of the Liberator.

The aircraft was a beast. The bomber's wings, fuselage, nose and tails were shaped by stringers, grids of support that formed a skeleton for the Liberator's aluminum-sheeted skin. Most of the Liberator's outer shell was one-tenth an inch or less thick. To wrap the bomber, those sheets were cut into long, 20-foot sections.

Nose to tail, each bomber consumed 4,200 square feet of aluminum. Five miles of wiring. 1.2 million parts. When a new bird rumbled off the line it was shiny and silver until it got the warpaint of its theater. Pinkish-gray for the desert. Battle drab for England.

Give me 50,000 warbirds, Roosevelt said. *We have to be ready.*

Sorenson fought off his nerves, tried not to think of the enormity of the problem the president had just asked him to solve. He took a deep breath and scribbled again.

It was not so different than an automobile. Many, many more parts — but still a mechanical system of gears, sheets of metal, bindings of welding, rivets and pulleys. He began to break the plane down into sections. Fuselage. Center wing. Nose turret. Tails. To build them in bulk numbers, each part built to the exact specifications of the piece before it, so they were interchangeable. To arrange all the parts in a line on one central floor. To roll out mass production assembly and cut man hours.

He drew and drew. The stacks of paper soon covered the floor.

The next morning, Sorenson handed his sketches to Edsel Ford.

"We'll need to construct an assembly plant larger than any before it," Sorenson said to his boss. "But I can build you a bomber an hour."

***

Two hours north of them, Grand Central Air Terminal was churning out pilots to fill those planes.

I can't believe they are paying me $75 a month for this, Dick thought. He had made it. He was on track to his fighter pilot dream. It was a Sunday evening at the flying school and my grandfather sat at a late-night meal with rows of other cadets. They dined at an abandoned casino near the airfield that the Army had converted into a mess hall. After the men came back from a weekend's leave of carousing, the Army rewarded them with plates full of ham, turkey and cake for a midnight meal before ordering them to their bunks.

Just like Roosevelt had pushed industry to begin building thousands of aircraft, he'd pushed the nation's civilian flying schools to start preparing men to fly them. The flying program established at Glendale's Grand Central Air Terminal was one of nine schools that sprung to action to quickly educate young men in air warfare. These civilian schools provided the first three months of elementary flight training. Hours of additional class-work in the airport's hangars covered navigation, engineering, radio and armament. Even with this intense focus, the young men these programs churned out would only have about 200 flying hours under their belts before they flew war missions for real.

Cadets had to be unmarried men who were at least 20 years old, but not older than 27. They had to be at least 5-foot-4, but could be no taller than 6-foot-2. They had to have 20/20 vision, and 20/20 hearing, and have a "well-formed, well-adjusted and coordinated physique."

If they hadn't completed two years of college they had to test in. The men were tested on both general and U.S. history, English grammar, geography, high algebra, trigonometry and elementary physics.

The U.S. history portion covered everything from "the discov-ery of the American continent to the present time." The general history section asked about "the history of ancient Greece and Rome, and the history of medieval Europe up to the discovery of America."

The program knew it was attractive, an opportunity to another life.

"A young man who has decided to follow aviation as his career and who has received the benefits of Army Air Corps flying training ... finds himself in a most favorable position," the Army wrote, in a manual it handed out to each cadet prospect. It also warned them that many of them would not make it.

"It is only natural that a number of flying cadets will, especially in the early stages of training, be found unsuited to become military pilots." Dick had made the cut. He was an Army Air Corps Flying Cadet, gold braid on his sleeve. He led parades in his hometown of Glendale and made his father proud. He soaked up the attention of the Hollywood Starlets Association, which doted on the young men with Sunday teas. He darted his PT-13 Stearman, the Army's open-air biplane, over California's skies. Dick relished circling wide on these routes, to come in low and hedge-hop over the homes of Hollywood actors.

"Once we had soloed, we were allowed to wear white scarves made out of parachute silk and were thrown into a swimming pool by our fellow cadets," Dick wrote.

He was boastful and thrilled, and found with flying that there was no more need for restraint. I paled a bit at the next few lines I knew he had Abuela type.

"We played like kings," he said. "I had been reunited with my girlfriend and it didn't take long for her to seduce me, in the back seat of my father's car, and in plain daylight. We had intercourse regularly after that."

His class went through three months of training and prepared for its first "wash" ride — a major milestone in the training program. The Air Corps required these test flights to weed out pilots who wouldn't progress to the next stage.

In the pages that would follow, the details of my grandfather's war would fight him. But this moment was a gift. His paragraphs were exact and full. What's more, he'd left me a news clip to go with it.

"I was scheduled for a routine wash ride with 1st Lt. Robert Lee Scott," he began.

Scott would later become a famous Flying Tiger and author of the book "God Is My Co-Pilot." That day, however, he was the instructor who took off with a student but landed without one.

My grandfather's silk scarf fluttered as he climbed into the Stearman. He looked up. That moment his daring, darting gray eyes betrayed him. Despite his bravado and dominance I could tell he was afraid. *If he failed, it would be in front of everyone.*

The wash ride was a straightforward test: pass and graduate to advanced flying; fail and wash out. Scott knew my grandfather was a skilled cadet. He didn't know my grandfather had made a fateful $5 bet.

Perhaps it was cover for fear of failure, perhaps it was sabotage. "I told the other cadets I had always wanted to use a parachute. I said that if there was the slightest indication that I might be washed out, I would bail out. Another cadet bet me that I wouldn't do it. I accepted the bet."

Dick taxied the Stearman to the runway and pushed the throttle to full, pulling the little yellow and blue bird of an airplane into flight.

The wash rides were not long; there was little time with so many pilots to review. Early in, Scott tested his cadet.

"We were about 400 feet in the air when Scott suddenly cut the throttle," Dick wrote.

This was expected. The Army Air Force wanted to see how each cadet would react to engine failure. It was terrifying but Dick thought: *I'm ready for this.*

Dick gripped the stick. It was his airplane. He was not afraid. The runway was behind them, but there was a field ahead. There was no need for panic. *Easy gliding distance ...*

"You're going to stall!!" Scott roared at this cocky son of a bitch through the gosports, plastic tubing that connected his angry instructor's voice to Dick's cold and bursting eardrums. "Are you trying to kill us both?!"

Scott slapped the stick forward pushing the nose down to pick up speed. Dick grimaced.

"I was sure I'd been washed out," he wrote.

The wash ride went on: Climb. Dip. Evade. My grandfather flew as he'd learned. But his head was wandering and his heart was pounding. How to save face? He could not land as a failure. So he looked down at his parachute.

"I told Lt. Scott I'd been unable to learn to execute a good, slow roll," he said.

They were chopping through the air over Glendale, flying at 4,000 feet. Scott saw a teachable moment for this arrogant cadet, and put the plane into a graceful and precise slow roll.

And at the top, my grandfather unfastened his safety belt and dropped to the Earth.

Scott was finishing the roll: *Did he really just feel that? He looked back over his shoulder to the empty seat and his heart pounded to his ears at the sight of the flapping safety belt.*

Dick was floating above Glendale, goggles pressed to his face. He squinted as the sun made a landing spot hard to see. He didn't want this sensation to end but in a quick click he remembered to put his hand on his groin then yanked the ripcord down, spilling silk parachute into the sky. He landed hard in a fig orchard.

Scott circled overhead to ensure his cadet was alive, then darted away back to the airfield. On the ground, a shocked fig orchard owner helped my grandfather hobble to a phone. Dick dialed his training commander.

"Sir, this is Cadet Harris. I've just fallen out of the airplane."

"My god! What happened to the plane?!" the commander replied.

A car rushed to my grandfather. He stretched out in back seat, wincing from his fractured vertebrae and ankle sprain. The car pulled up to the base, where he could see his commander waiting in the driveway to check on his injuries.

Dick's dim-witted fellow cadet was outside too. When the car door opened, the cadet pushed between the two of them to hand Dick five dollars.

"I didn't think you'd really do it!"

The elder Harris first heard the news on the radio at home. And that evening, "that Harris kid" again made *The Glendale News-Press*.

"Cadet Captain Harris Falls from Airplane, Lands by Parachute."

A Board of Inquiry followed. Dick admitted his bailout was no accident. Scott testified that prior to the "fall" Dick had passed his wash ride; his reaction to the cut throttle had been the right one. With a sigh of relief, Dick learned he would be reprimanded but returned to flying status. He realized then just how much he'd risked, how he'd almost wrecked his chance to fly.

His stunt made the monthly Army Air Cadets newsletter that July. In typical military fashion, it put a somewhat positive spin on the incident.

Flying Cadet R.C. Harris of Class 40-H at the primary training detachment at Glendale, Calif., became the detachment's first emergency parachute jumper when he accidentally dislodged the catch on his safety belt during a check ride with Lt. R.L. Scott and in the midst of a snap roll found himself in mid-air with no airplane to hang onto. The cool-headed Cadet, who reported that he had no sensation of falling, but merely seemed to be floating in mid-air, calmly pulled the rip cord, stowed it away in his pocket in keeping with Army tradition, and in due course of time landed in a soft plowed field.

Hitchhiking to San Fernando nearby, he startled Commanding Officer, Captain K.P. McNaughton, with a phone call, in which he reported, "Sir, this is Cadet Harris. I just fell out of an airplane."

Cadet Harris, whose home is in Glendale, Calif., thus preserved the "no accident" record of his detachment.

Several weeks later, Washington weighed in. The Board of Inquiry's decision was reversed by headquarters, which was not amused by the lack of respect this cadet had shown for its program. My grandfather's Army Air Corps Flying Cadet days were over. In July 1940, he was honorably discharged from the military before the U.S. ever entered the war.

7

Purple Hearts

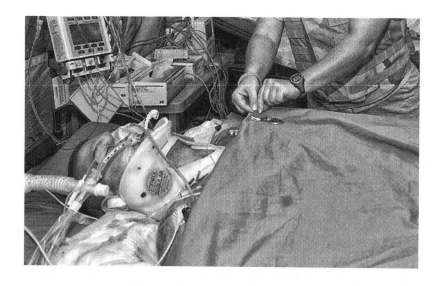

San Angelo, Texas, 2003; and Balad, Iraq, September 11, 2004
I beat Wurm, Cortez, Holmes and Kolfage home by a couple of ugly months that included a break-up and a move out, when my D.C. boyfriend snooped through my laptop and learned about Wurm. I was already wildly unbalanced. The act of garbage-bagging two carloads of personal belongings

and spinning once more into reinvention made things worse. I went to Abuela's house seeking refuge; I came home with my grandfather's text. It was a good start, but most of the rest of me was just an unpredictable mess.

So that July when the Goodfellow crew was headed home to Texas I got very hopeful. I yearned to hit the "reset" button. Reconnecting with Wurm, Cortez, Kolfage and Holmes could help me get back to a point of stability, I thought.

An irrational plan was hatched: When they arrived back, I'd go to San Angelo to welcome them. I somehow expected that rejoining these returned airmen would be where I was supposed to be. It was the only plan I had. I flew into town under the guise of needing to meet with my editors, and with the convenient timing that Goodfellow's 17th Security Forces Squadron was coming home. I flew into that city with no situational awareness or common sense. San Angelo was also very glad to have its men home and had a lot of catching up to do. As did Angelo State, the city's college full of pretty women who were ready to party with their handsome uniformed heroes.

I spent the day in our *San Angelo Standard-Times* newsroom waiting for the night to arrive. I reached out and Kolfage answered, I was so glad to have plans. After work I sped to my hotel, an economy Best Western on the outskirts of town and ran through a shower. I thought and rethought about what to wear. In Iraq and Kuwait there'd been no burden of choice. I had the camouflage, or I had a red sleeveless T-shirt. The red T-shirt and jeans was for fancy nights, the drab tan camo-wear, for all else. But now I had five different outfits crammed into a suitcase, each judged against the important criteria of being attractive without revealing how hard I was trying.

I was ready. Excited. I sat on my flat, scratchy Best Western economy hotel bed waiting for their call. My hair was done. I had too much makeup on because I kept applying and reapplying it, so the moment we first saw each other, I would look better than perfect.

Those first hours alone I told myself *good. My hair wasn't cooperating in this heat. It was good that they are late.*

I raced through another shower and blew it dry fast, again.

They are coming, they're just guys, and they have a lot going on, but they are coming. And Wurm ... what would that be like? I pushed past the instinct that knew our last interaction was awkward and wrong. It warned me that until now I hadn't really missed him, I just needed to miss someone. I played out the night in my mind. I didn't let myself think about how late it was getting. I did not let myself think about how I was alone in this hotel room, with a rattling window air conditioner unit and basic cable. I embraced the bad hotel cable instead, watching for funny scenes I could tell the guys about. When it was too late for us to get dinner I finally gave in and went out for drive-through fast food, then sped back to my room. When they were still not there, I worried I'd missed them because I'd left to get a burger.

Maybe they meant we'd go out late night, like in college ...

But there was nothing. No call. No answer to the scarce handful of texts I sent, asking what the plans were. I didn't want to send too many; I didn't want to seem like I was bothering them. But what if my texts hadn't gone through? What if one of them had lost their phone? *There was too much at stake not to text again, just one more time.* But the text went unanswered into that painful quiet void. Then there was nothing left. Nothing to distract me, no more excuses. So in the last feint hint of night, I drew the room's first-floor blinds. I did not want anyone in the parking lot to see me, this mess of a girl doubling over in heaving sobs on a scratchy Best Western bed when I finally understood that no one was coming at all.

"Sorry ... he and Kolfage had to take a road trip to San Antonio," Cortez told me the next day about why I never heard from Wurm. Cortez was so kind he didn't have to tell me they weren't alone, and he didn't press: *What were you thinking.*

What was I thinking, I asked, unsteadily. *This isn't yours.* Without seeing anyone I wished them all well and turned my rental car toward the airport. I thought, if this journey was confusing for me, it had to be for them too. It just took one bad night in a West Texas motel room to learn the blunt, hard truth: This wasn't a path toward home at all.

Instead, I persuaded my editors to send me back to Iraq. I went not only to report on reconstruction but to move past my first experience there. To understand war through eyes that were not naive like they were on my first run. To find a way to keep both war's heroics and its ugliness at a controllable, discrete distance. But once I arrived back in Iraq, I saw war was in control there, and nothing else. The country was decentralized and disorganized and tethered to its past, even as it forced its way to a different future. There were increasingly complex tribal rivalries, political secrets, unwritten rules and ever changing footholds. What war hissed to me, to the hundreds of thousands of Americans there, to everyone: *This isn't yours.*

I saw this lack of accountability play out in different ways. For many, there was the attitude of *"what happens on deployment ...."* Villas overflowed with hard liquor. Soldiers drank until they passed out in the lounge chairs strewn around Saddam's Republican Palace pool, eventually spurring General Order No. 1: No drinking. Officers asked to marry their Iraqi villa maids. A fluorescent green sludge of trash oozed through Sadr City, past kids kicking U.S. Agency for International Development soccer balls. I saw Iraqi passports burn and black trash bags filled with U.S. $20 and $100 bills disappear; they were loaded into the back seats of black uparmored SUVs that moved the cash north to new Iraqi allies.

In that short trip I also reconnected with Scharf, who was still there, still assigned to getting Iraq's schools built even though its refineries really could have used her expertise. I worked with her to expose shameful school repair performance by America's major defense contractors, which got me temporarily banned from the contractor-operated cafeterias. Oh well. I didn't mind being back to MREs.

I saw heartbreaking acts of goodwill, as individual soldiers brought positive change to the lives of individual Iraqis. On one run, soldiers intervened on the behalf of deaf seamstresses who'd been mistreated by their boss. Those women now saw their first glimmer of a happier future, and adored the troops. I saw completed, pretty schools too, their walls painted pink and green, with eager young Iraqi schoolgirls smiling behind new desks. I saw hope in the eyes of so many soldiers, when the Iraqi kids would come racing to them for fun and the expectation of a sweet. *This is going slower than we'd thought it would,* the troops would say. *But we need to stay. It's working ...*

But there was a sinister quiet undercurrent too, a deepening frustration over the cultural divide between Iraqi and U.S. expectations. As it twisted and turned with distrust and greed, I saw masses of people on both sides realize that time overseas meant a fattened bank account if you played your cards right. *There was no reason to hurry.* Distrust on motive spread, protests at the massive military gates now barricading the Green Zone spread. Even good intentions failed, because few believed in good intentions anymore. I tried to connect my translator to someone in the military, so his colleague, another Iraqi, could collect a reward. The military had started printing leaflets that said the U.S. would pay for loose munitions to get them off the street. Over a meal at Pizzaria Napoli – a bizarre Baghdad café that used what looked like hotdog slices instead of pepperoni, my translator handed me the blue and white flyer and asked for help.

Surely we could figure this out, I thought. It would be a win to get those weapons off the street. I brought the paper to the company commander, Maj. Michael Maguire.

"He has a weapons cache," I said of my translator's friend. He'd told me they included shoulder-fired rocket launchers, and this anonymous Iraqi wanted to exchange them for the reward. Understandably, he couldn't drive them up to the Green Zone gate.

Maguire pondered this. It would be awesome to secure those weapons.

But what if it was a trap?

Was there any way to prove it wasn't?

Maguire had been down this road before. The Iraq Survey Group and the 75th Exploitation Task Force had sent his men on wild goose chases to secure weaponry they never found. Link-up points would change mid-mission. There would be no Iraqi contact at the designated time.

"Inshallah," their Iraqi counterparts would say. Which sometimes meant "God willing it will happen." It often meant "it's not on me if it doesn't."

There wasn't enough proof. There wasn't enough trust. The Americans would not risk exposing their men; the Iraqi would not drive the cache to the gate. The mission was a no-go; the weapons went nowhere.

Whatever objective had created a fleeting sense of unity in 2003 was now drunk and stumbling for any open door. Iraq was no place to reinvent, to understand war better, or even to shed light on my first trip. This was another country now.

I learned about the "Mrs." — other female reporters who had latched on to soldiers, and decided that must be the way things were in war. So without fanfare I made my own new friend. He was a good soldier I slept with without emotion in the back of a transport van in a Green Zone parking lot. I did it because I could. I wanted to see war the way I thought I was supposed to see it. I wanted to move past the idealistic grip that remained from my first ride in. I tried to be as detached and blunt as war apparently was. I did my job, and I came home.

I wasn't lost. But I wasn't sure I ever wanted to see Iraq again. Several months later, Wurm reached out across the distance. "Have you heard about Kolfage?"

***

Sept. 11, 2004: A streak of dust and sunlight pushed Kolfage awake. He blinked to relieve dry eyes and with a squint and a grunt Kolfage stretched out of his Air Force tent bunk at Balad Air Base. Time to hit the gym.

It was shortly after 2 p.m.

Kolfage didn't have to be there. He and Cortez were both on a second deployment. They had been assigned to Kuwait-based duty, but then Cortez's name was picked in a lottery to send additional Air Force security forces forward to protect Balad's flight line. There was no way Kolfage would let Cortez go back to Iraq without him. He looked for someone he could scare into switching, to convince that Iraq was too dangerous, so that he could take his spot and be with Cortez. He found a new kid, a soon-to-be dad. Kolfage growled: *You might lose your legs.* He scared the guy into staying back, and Kolfage got his place next to Cortez.

Cortez and Kolfage were only on their first weeks at Balad, but they already had a system. Night shift. Sleep. Gym. Eat. Repeat. "We did everything together," Cortez said.

On this day Kolfage woke first. He put on his shorts and a T-shirt and shuffled out of the tent that he, Cortez and a handful of other men shared outside of Balad's flight line. Cortez was slower to rise. As Kolfage opened the tent flap, he asked Cortez if he wanted bottled water, and got only a muffled, yawning reply. Then he stepped out into the sunlight and turned left in the sand toward the gym tent.

There was no "duck and cover," no "giant voice" — those sirens installed all over Iraq and Afghanistan in the following years that gave troops a four to eight-second headstart to run for a bunker and escape incoming fire.

This was 2004, and Balad wasn't expecting the 107 mm rocket shell that exploded five feet from Linebacker 10's babyfaced airman.

The blast flattened Kolfage to the sand. His eyes were stuck open but he only saw darkness as his body and hair disappeared into a cloud of sand and smoke. Each of his senses knocked to black.

I'm dreaming, Kolfage thought, *those malaria pills give crazy, crazy dreams.*

Then his senses raced back screaming *you've been hit.* Hearing returned first. Kolfage shuddered at the wail of a base siren. He heard a soldier who'd been not 10 feet away start to shriek.

Oh shit ... wasn't I just walking?

Next came taste. Kolfage sensed sandy wet grit in his mouth. Then he smelled smoke.

Oh shit oh shit.

Sight returned. *Is my hand blown off? Oh shit oh shit I am hurt bad.* Kolfage opened his lungs and yelled for help. He tried to move but Cortez and nearby soldiers were already on him, they stuffed muscled hands and forearms and towels into Kolfage's lower bleeding half to try and save his life.

Kolfage looked at Cortez crazy with blood on him. He pushed against his battle buddy and yelled for Cortez to let him see his legs. Cortez put his bloody hand over Kolfage's eyes to protect him from deadly shock.

The attack and response was 30 seconds, start-stop. Kolfage screamed for water and Cortez dumped a bottle on his face and mouth as medics arrived screaming *don't do that you'll kill him.* Kolfage slumped and told him he was tired. Cortez slapped him hard again and again to piss him off and into consciousness.

The medics slammed him onto a blue body board and it was not until that very second Kolfage's last sense returned. He started crying out and cussing in agonized pain. Every nerve in his body convulsed with panicked throbs, searching for his two missing legs and missing right arm. They were there but they weren't. His hips led to a mash of bright red blood and tissue left pulsing under flapping pieces of skin. His right arm was shredded bone and more skin after the bend in his elbow. Cortez helped the medics push all of it, the flesh and bone and tissue from Balad's sandy ground up onto the body board, all those ripped-up pieces of a young man they now raced to keep together.

Kolfage screamed as the ambulance sped toward the hospital tent. He begged for morphine which the medics could not give. He cursed loudly at the medical staff who met the gurney with absolute shock.

And then, nothing. Kolfage passed out.

***

Cortez still had his hands on Kolfage's wounds when the medics finally separated them. It gave Cortez a moment of reality. He looked at the ground. He saw things. Bloody things. He pushed away from them and jumped beside Kolfage in the ambulance.

When the medical team charged the gurney through Balad's field hospital Cortez was left outside. He stood by the hospital's tent flaps, wondering why he was wearing his buddy's bloody hat.

The base issued a call for blood. Within minutes a line of airmen, Marines, sailors and soldiers formed around the hospital's sandbags and canvas. Some came on bikes, some just came running as soon as they heard the call.

It was barely 3 p.m.

Cortez waited out the news. Kolfage survived the first surgery. *We had to amputate,* the doctors said.

He stood watch through the night. Cortez endured as people gave more support than he could stand. His team gathered. The chaplain hovered. A bunch of other people were just ... there.

Some minutes he'd crouch. Some minutes he'd stand, or walk in the sliver of light seeping from the hospital tent. Cortez waited. And overnight, Balad's medical team saved Kolfage's life. He was stabilized to fly. Word went out: Kolfage would be evacuated immediately on a massive C-5 Galaxy. The men and women of Balad Air Base who had lined up to give blood shifted into a line to salute Kolfage's path to the plane. They stood, some silent, some cheering support as the ambulance slowly drove an unconscious Kolfage to the flight line.

Cortez had 1,000 thoughts running through his head as the

ambulance approached the plane.

You can say goodbye, he'd been told. Cortez was given special permission to approach the gurney before it was lifted into the C-5's hold.

Cortez walked up to his friend. Kolfage was intubated, his neck was in a brace. His face was barely visible through gauze and bruises and wiring.

Cortez thought of all they had shared, serving in these dangerous lands. Cortez knew this was the last time he would see his friend for a long time. He remembered what they used to shout to stay motivated during long night watches and when they pushed each other at the gym.

Cortez leaned in close to Kolfage's face and repeated the words.

We live together. We fight together. We die together. We Band of Brothers.

***

Two weeks later, compassionate doctors eased Kolfage into news he vaguely grasped as he drifted in and out of morphine-infused consciousness at Walter Reed Army Medical Center.

Oh that really did happen. My legs are gone.

I visited Kolfage at Walter Reed shortly after, because Wurm had reached out.

The room was dim, with blinds halfway drawn across the lone window. Kolfage was propped on pillows, a blanket covered him from his waist down. It went flat after his hips, except for small ridges of fabric caused by a dozen lines of tubing that connected him to fluids and medicine.

His arm was now a white bandaged nub that seeped yellow puss.

This room was the exact opposite of the Baghdad I'd last seen. It was the real price and real life of war. As we said our first "hellos" in a year, I looked into the hollow and drugged eyes of my friend and wondered if he knew he was smiling.

"You can sit on the bed," she said. It was a direct but almost challenging welcome from his girlfriend, a pretty 20-year-old who Kolfage had dated on and off since high school.

Kolfage had lived in Hawaii back then. He'd been a sandy, 15-year-old punk of a kid who was hanging out on an apartment balcony with friends when he saw her riding a skateboard and called down. When the Air Force moved her family to Texas he'd followed. Then he decided to enlist.

When the phone rang where she was staying in San Antonio during his second deployment she couldn't stop screaming until someone could convince her Kolfage was still alive.

I sat on the bed. I don't know what exactly I said to her or to Kolfage. I remember it was a muting task to open my mouth because every crutch I used to reconnect — "How's it going? What have you been up to?" — was an embarrassing failure. I knew how Kolfage was. He was one-half. He was right in front of me. I still asked. What the hell else do you do? I asked about the hospital food.

"I just started eating solids again," he said. "The food sucks," she corrected.

I asked if his parents were OK. I asked what I could do to help. That one was the trigger. His young girlfriend had the weight of the world on her shoulders, but said nothing. How do you complain about the stress and the fear and the responsibilities that did not exist three weeks ago, *when you have both of your legs and your arm and you did not serve our country in Iraq?* Kolfage never, ever said this. But it was in her head, in her mind, in her heart. It was in the eyes of every new "friend," all those doctors and nurses and hospital coordinators who would make small talk of their own: "How are *you* doing?" The first few times when she dared show fraying she saw the flicker of judgment. Of pity. And she quickly learned to just smile and say she was fine.

Instead she focused. She moved back and forth from checking on his bandages, like the nurses had taught her, to staring at her phone for the 100th time, wondering if this next number she'd been told to dial would finally get them the support they needed. Access to cash. A place for her to crash while Kolfage healed. She had nowhere to go, she didn't want to be anywhere but here. At night she curled up beside Kolfage on the bed, her shampooed hair a soft and welcome respite from the medical smell of the sheets.

When I asked what I could do to help, it was a hollow offer like so many others would be. She quickly shut me down; in even the few weeks since the attack she'd learned to read a real offer from an empty one. It was a survival instinct.

She was right, there was not much I could do. But I could take my notebook and my pen and four weeks after Kolfage was hit the best thing I could do was to write and write and get their story on our wire.

A few days after "United for the Journey" hit our newspapers they married. With no dress and no ring they were joined by a Walter Reed chaplain. They were a young man and a young woman who sat together on Kolfage's hospital bed with no legs and no right hand. He put his left hand in hers and they vowed to face this unknown together.

8

The Search

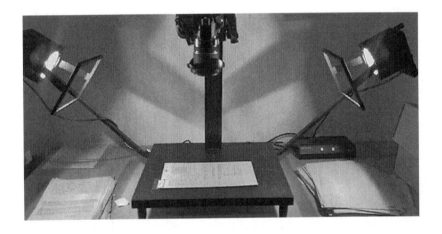

N *ational Archives 2005-2007, and Dick and Terry's path to war, 1942*

Right about the time Kolfage was healing at Walter Reed I stopped being able to report on politics. Which was unfortunate, since I was still a political reporter.

The nonsense and the pettiness and the battle of spin made me sick inside; I no longer had the heart for the Washington game. But I wasn't sure I could go back to Baghdad either. War had become a business. The nation's budget for it tripled and the number of men and women who saw profit in patriotism skyrocketed. I took a job reporting on defense from the industry side, but that was short lived. When I stepped into those mammoth defense shows I just wanted to leave, they were rooms of white smiles and floor displays of missiles and the newest technology, all to "support the warfighter."

Maybe all of them really believed that. The problem was, I didn't.

So, I was busy floundering professionally. There were so many doors open because of Iraq but I did a shit job of marketing myself to any of them because I couldn't shake the unease that walking through them made me a war profiteer too. I was trapped. I couldn't define myself outside of war anymore. But I couldn't find a comfortable role within it, either.

Instead, I tried again with my grandfather.

After he was discharged from the Army, Dick wasted no time looking for an alternate path to war — through the Royal Canadian Air Force. He was assigned not as a fighter pilot, but as a multi-engine bomber pilot. He shipped overseas and flew twin-engine Blenheims over Berlin.

But not before many more one-night stands. "Canadian girls were missing their men," he said.

Then Pearl Harbor ignited the nation and the U.S. Army Air Forces called my grandfather home. It wanted every able-bodied pilot to fill its ranks, even the unrestrained ones it had previously discharged.

The Army sent him back to California.

Go teach, the Army told him. Multi-engine instructors were badly needed.

No, no, no, he stammered.

I will not sit out this war.

I'll show them, my grandfather said.

"Back in Lemoore, I was to gain a new nickname: 'Windsock Harris,'" he said.

Dick was proud of the annoyance he became. He could not believe the Army had pulled him all the way back home.

This is backwards and wrong, he thought.

"I dived on an auxiliary field tower and came away with the windsock embedded in my left wing. Since this made turns difficult, I landed in a cultivated field straight in front of me. The farmer came out and gave me hell. I said, 'Mister, aren't you glad to see me alive?'"

"Then I flew down to San Bernardino. I dove on my father's ranch house and scared the hell out of every human being and every animal within half a mile of radius. Farmers had no difficulty getting my plane's number. I scooted through the treetops and finally landed at Ontario. There I called my father and asked him to pick me up. Of course, when I got back to Lemoore, I was 'on report.' I buzzed daily, and broke every single flying regulation as often as I could. And every Thursday, without fail, I reported to the Director of Operations and requested transfer to combat."

He got his wish. Lemoore, Calif., wanted nothing more to do with him.

After that, I knew he trained in Sioux City, Iowa, with movie star Jimmy Stewart. I didn't know this because he named a unit. I knew it because he had Abuela type up a sheet about the formal ball that Jimmy Stewart couldn't attend, because "he would have been mobbed by all the girls." Dick on the other hand was miffed that he'd spent the night in the same bed as his date but she never took off her ballgown. I knew his first destination was England, but I didn't know a town. I just knew that it was near Greenwich and that he often had his "pick of the lot" of the girls when he visited the private bottle clubs in London.

There wasn't a single group or squadron in the text to help me. He named one group commander in England, a "Colonel Townsend." I hit the Internet enough to know that no one by that name existed. For now, my grandfather was going nowhere.

***

At least I knew where Terry was. After the Naval Academy kicked him out he joined the Merchant Marines. But war from the sea was too distant, too detached for my great uncle. There was one option left: infantry.

But the principles and expectations his father had drilled into Terry made basic infantry impossible. *He was destined for more, he should be pushed for more.*

It was August 1942. The U.S. and European powers had just two decades of warplane experience under their belts. America had never dropped a parachuted man from a plane into war.

But now several countries were looking at "sky soldiers" as a new tactic to break through enemy defenses. The United States could not afford to be left behind. It would have two divisions:

The 82nd Airborne Division was activated Aug. 15, 1942. A day later, Aug. 16, 1942, the 101st Airborne Division was activated at Camp Claiborne, La.

On Aug. 17, 1942, Terry reported for duty.

As he was processed in, Terry was asked if he was interested in volunteering for this new force: *Do you think you have what it takes to be a paratrooper?* Volunteers for that duty were rare; it was an unknown. Ride an airplane and fall into battle? *That sounded like a death sentence.* So, of course, by the end of the week Terry was on a train to Toccoa, Ga. He was assigned to the 101st Airborne Division, 506th Parachute Infantry Regiment,

2nd Battalion, Easy Company.

Many good authors and HBO's dedication have expertly captured the tales of these storied men — Terry, Lt. Dick Winters, Sgt. Don Malarkey, Staff Sgt. Bill Guanere and the rest of Easy Company. They have preserved the memory of Toccoa; of the dreaded six mile ruck up and back the mountain of Currahee. Of the cruelty of no water and the spitefulness of spaghetti dinners as their Company commander, Capt. Herbert Sobel, forged these men into iron by shouting as they put forkfuls of pasta in their mouths that Easy would run that mountain *right now,* again.

Terry didn't have to be a Paratrooper. None of these men did. But once Terry got to Easy, there was nowhere else he could be. In December 1942 he earned his Jump Wings.

Terry's penchant to compete was a good fit for Sobel's strict standards and by spring 1943 Terry was promoted to staff sergeant.

Terry's penchant to challenge authority ... was not such a good pairing.

He and Easy Company shipped to England in Summer 1943, but it was an uneasy ride. Stephen Ambrose has immortalized the loss of trust and simmering anger the men of Easy had developed by then against Sobel, who had lost their respect with bad decisions and a lack of basic decency. Worse, the men had become certain that Sobel would get them killed.

On Oct. 30, 1943, this came to a head, and fans of "Band of Brothers" know the rest. Terry was furious at the injustice he perceived in the treatment of his executive officer, Lt. Dick Winters, of the trumped-up court martial Sobel put Winters through out of spite.

This is wrong, my great-uncle bristled.

Terry was one of two staff sergeants who began to rally the

other NCOs.

Let's turn in our stripes ... it's the only way.

Mutiny.

The court martial paperwork embarrassed the whole regiment; there had to be punishment. Sobel was removed from command of Easy. Terry was transferred to Baker Company and demoted to the rank of private.

Dad will think I failed again, Terry feared.

He was pulled from Easy, eight months before D-Day.

***

Sioux City. That was where Dick's war story went cold, and my search for him began. I looked at his memoirs again. They led nowhere. His pages flowed with bravado. But not a single damn unit.

Where are you? I asked, frustrated.

It turned out that if you needed to finish your grandfather's war story, you had to go to the National Archives campus in College Park, Md.

The building is lesser known than its more famous sister, the National Archives in downtown Washington, D.C.

At the downtown Archives, tourists lined up for hours to see the documents that founded our nation. The Archives in College Park, on the other hand, sheltered the 200 years of U.S. paperwork behind them.

In this gleaming white building, raw history could be touched, photographed, leafed through. Inside I lost track of time. Sometimes I looked up and it was snowing. Other times it rained. Only when darkness fell did I remember it was time to go home. I wore white gloves and tenderly handled mimeographed sheets

70 years old that crumbled at my touch.

I didn't see a single sheet with my grandfather's name. Never known for his patience, or for letting death stop him from telling me what to do, he looked up, foot tapping.

Send me to war, he said.

I'm trying, I smarted back.

Each of these archival trips became more obsessive, a one-way narrative of lonely page turning.

My grandfather, at first great company on these dives into history, got frustrated.

Why don't you see me?

Were your string of conquests the only thing you had to show for your war? I snapped at him.

Were we so different? he sassed back. He turned away, with a whisper: *You'll learn it doesn't matter.*

Then he left me to the stacks.

I was trying to be different. Trying to get back to "right." After Kolfage was hit I started a master's degree in war studies. I left journalism for the Government Accountability Office, a place where I could work toward making the battlefield the place I thought it should be for the men and women fighting on it. I became serious with the most reliable man I'd met, a guy with blue-green eyes and an Irish smile. I looked at the instability of the world, the insurgencies, the stop losses, my friend's injuries and the unfairness of it all and said: *Just be bloody grateful for this normal, comfortable life.* I prepared for marriage, trying with my whole soul to become something good, post-Iraq. If I could only let it go.

My grandfather's memoirs sat untouched for months, partly because every time I read about another of his war conquests, I felt my cheeks burn in discomfort about my own. Truth, I could get nowhere with them. I was stretched too thin, too busy being so many things and I wasn't sure how many of them actually fit. It was almost a frantic determination: *If I plowed ahead, fast, all of this would stick.*

Through it all, I kept going back to California, prodding Abuela, looking for clues. She sewed ring bearer pillows; she pushed me not to give up. She signed government paperwork that granted me access to Dick's official military records, hoping there would be answers for me there. Every military member who has served has a file in the government's system, and a lot of those records were housed at the National Personnel Records Center in St. Louis. But with World War II requests, there was often only terrible news on the other end.

Many months later, the St. Louis notification mailed to so many WWII families arrived at my door: *Sorry, the 1973 fire destroyed whatever records we had.*

Challenge is life, my grandfather scolded, then jumped into an unknown bomber and took off without me.

9

Rose Leigh

S *cience Hill, Ky. 1943*

The first U.S. heavy bomber response to Pearl Harbor took place just two days after the surprise attack. U.S. B-17s that had survived a separate Japanese attack in the Philippines bombed advancing Japanese warships on Dec. 9, 1941, sinking one.

Thousands of B-24s would fill the skies in the next 18 months. But that December 1941, the Liberator was just starting production. Only 33 left the assembly line.

Due to Sorenson's fevered sketches, that was about to change. So were the lives of 42,000 workers who would migrate to Ypsilanti, Mich., and become a part of this war machine. Ford's Willow Run.

A petite brunette named Rose Leigh Abbott was about to become one of them.

***

It was summer 1943. Rose sat at the rural bus stop of her Science Hill, Ky., hometown. She was in pants, shirt tucked tight, job ads in hand. Five-year-old Connie and 2-year-old Troy were back at her aging parents' farmhouse, waiting for their mother's next move. They were all she had in the world and she was so afraid.

On the bench beside her, another young mother, traveling with her kids. Rose looked down — those children's shoes were held together with canning jar rings.

Rose closed her eyes in stress. *I've got to get out of here. That can't be me.*

She knew she was handy with tools, the tomboy of her peers.

Once she got to nearby Somerset's small town square, she asked about mechanics' jobs.

Sorry love, there's nothing for you here.

She heard this again and again until she felt something inside

her about to break. It was a slow suffocation to stare down a life of closed doors. Exhausted and for the moment defeated, she walked to the town diner. She dared not buy lunch; who knew how long her money would last. She opted only for lemonade, and overheard two older men chatting at the counter.

There's machining work in Michigan. Ford's hiring thousands.

A few weeks later, Rose and her two kids were carefully stepping off a bus. She carried Troy in her arms and Connie dragged a little suitcase as the three got their first look at Ypsilanti.

Rose's first gaze was not a good one. In every direction she saw endless golden fields and dotted farmhouses. For a second she panicked. *I've made a huge mistake! This is exactly like Science Hill.* But her eyes caught on to a ribbon of bodies — men and women like her carrying everything they owned in small suitcases. Her eyes panned the ribbon, tracing the people until her gaze was halted by a giant factory. Ford's Willow Run.

They joined the swell. Rose couldn't even see the end of the building. *It was 3,000 feet long.* Inside, Sorenson's hotel-room sketches of mass production for bomber assembly thundered to life.

It only took a few days to get settled in. Rose found a nearby farming family willing to board her children and rented a bed for herself in the Quonset hut barracks. Those metal domed huts ran up and down Willow Run's 7,000-foot runways, a perfect perch for workers to watch their finished Liberators take first flight.

Rose was assigned an employee card and a start date. First she had to complete two weeks of training in the schoolhouse. Ford was going to teach her and thousands of others who walked through its 42-foot factory doors how to build a bomber an hour. Rose was already ahead of many of her classmates, male and female. A lifetime of necessity as the third youngest child in a family of nine kids had taught her how to fix everything from the clothing on her back to the family car. As soon as she was old enough, she tagged after her father to help him as he worked on construction sites. So in many ways Willow Run felt like home. Sorenson's sketches had simplified the Liberator's construction into 70 major sub-assemblies. Each would be built at stations located on a long track that carried the bombers through the factory like a snake. The very tip of the bomber's nose was station 1A. At station 13, workers built bomb racks.

Start to finish, the assembly line was more than a mile long. Almost 90 bombers in some stage of production fed into it on any given day. Wings. Engines. Tails. Then, in the final stages, that main assembly line branched into four, where each bomber began its final 18-day journey from parts to flying warbird.

In those four final tracked lines, hundreds of workers climbed into and around each aluminum shell. They climbed ladders and cranes to lift and secure the three-blade propellers onto the shafts of Pratt & Whitney engines — each metal cone large enough for workers to sit upright. Workers roped together miles of aluminum coil through the hollows in each wing and fed them through the floor of the fuselage. They wove that metal roping past tubing for hydraulics and past canisters of life-saving oxygen at altitude. They bent their knees and lifted large rubber fuel bladders onto their backs and into the bombers' wings. And in moments of tired pride and rest, they leaned back against the Liberator's 4 ½-foot-tall tires; the rubber edges pressed gently against their shoulders.

The last few days were the best. The four lines merged to two; then each bomber could finally stretch the full length of its 110-foot wingspan and roll off the tracks and pulleys, tugged onto the tarmac for the first time.

Every other day, a new, incomplete frame tracked up the line to Rose's workstation. The hull sheets were shiny, perfect, spotless. Rose took her position alongside four other factory workers on either side of long sheets of endless pre-drilled holes. The fuselage alone required 126,000 rivets to hold it together.

On one side, Rose hoisted a riveting gun; on the other her co-worker ensured the metal pins and holes were aligned. Rose squeezed the trigger until the pins pushed through the shaft and popped metal on metal; sealed. Then on to the next rivet. They had a day and a half to finish this frame, before another aircraft rolled up to them. They were to move fast, but not faster than what was safe. *Bent aluminum was lost time.* These rhythmic movements shaped and formed the body of the bomber. By the time each frame finished its procession through Willow Run and rolled toward the open hangar gates, more than 313,000 rivets would bind the bomber's plating to seats, engines to wings, rudders to tails.

There was not much to do inside the aircraft in terms of furnishing; the Liberator was built for its gun power. The two large windows near the back, for the right and left waist gunners, were just large holes in the plane, each cut out for 65-pound, Browning .50-caliber M2 machine guns that swung wide to fire. The Liberator had 10 of these guns. Each warplane would be loaded with almost 5,000 bullets to feed them: 1,200 rounds of ammunition for the nose turret gun; 800 rounds for the top turret; 600 rounds for the tail. Then 1,000 rounds for the bottom turret and another 1,000 for those .50-cals mounted on the large windows at the waist.

The belly of the bomber was a sliding pair of aluminum bomb bay doors that rolled halfway up each side. The Liberator could carry two 4,000-pound bombs, eight 1,000-pound bombs, a collection of 250-pound or 500-pound bombs, or any number of combinations in between.

At her place alongside the bomber, Rose felt like she could exhale for the first time in her life. There was nothing Willow Run didn't give her: tools, training and resolve; purpose, patriotism and camaraderie. On Fridays, a larger salary than she'd dare dream. In moments off, she walked the line in awe.

She didn't mind that her male peers didn't quite get her. "Rose, grab me a left handed wrench, will you love?" the foreman teased.

Rose began to blush and couldn't keep herself from responding. "There's no such thing!"

The next day, Rose's work was inspected. Hands ran over the bolted seams, checking the quality of her work before the aluminum shell was tracked to the next station and a new one rolled up to her post.

It was a door to opportunity, a path to a new life. But the Liberator was more than that. It was built as a tomb for Hitler. It was the pride of Rose Leigh.

10

Rock Bottom

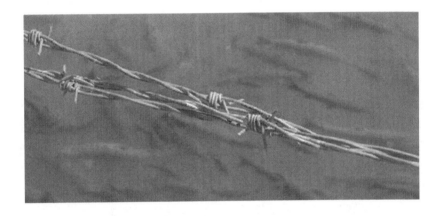

B*aghdad, Iraq 2009*

By 2009 I was married, but I shouldn't have been. My husband should have been married, just not to me. We stood together at the curbside passenger drop-off at Dulles

International Airport. I pulled my backpack from the back of his SUV. We said all the right words — the "I love yous." The "I'll miss yous." But they were half-hearted. Too hard to say; too hard not to say. The words fell empty on the pavement.

I was headed back to Iraq, as a government auditor this time. The military was through the surge and President Barack Obama had directed the final drawdown of U.S. troops. I was there with the GAO to assess those plans. But I had to get through this terrible goodbye first.

I tried to avoid this.

On a crisp fall walk in late 2004 — the earliest days of our relationship, I turned to my future husband and said, "I am going to try hard to protect you from myself."

In his typical mild way, he looked at me a bit confused, but shrugged, smiled and didn't dig further.

I didn't trust my own heart: Everyone else seemed to be happy; what was wrong with me? I told myself the sooner I let go and got on the same ride everyone else was so grateful for, the better off I'd be.

I did. I let go of all of it. I put my heart in a practical box, where I thought I could maintain course with a good man and prepare to have kids. I practiced, really hard, at being happy.

Colin Hay has a heartbreaking song, "Waiting for my real life to begin." On that disorienting first trip into the desert, all of life's extraneous noise got ripped away. It was an addictive clean feeling that was just as fleeting as it was intense.

I spent the next several years stumbling around reaching again for that rush. But it was nowhere to be found; not back with the men I'd first gone in with, not in the desert. It was a purity that blindsided me when I first experienced it, and then became less tactile and less true each time I thought about that first trip in.

But there was a competing feeling, too. It was discomforting to realize I'd felt so alive in a place so riddled with loss. More, that I'd been able to leave without paying the price so many others did. I began to question if I treated war like something that could be visited in denial, like a junkie. Instead I worked hard to get on an alternate path.

By that time, the war had come home. Soldiers suffered chemical burns in their lungs and cancerous tumors in their brains from burn pits. IED blasts left life-long migraines. Failed marriages left returning forces with emptied joint bank accounts.

I'd suffered none of that. I'd been one of the lucky ones. From a crass outsider's point of view I wouldn't argue if they said that war looked like it had been just a big adventure for a very unrealistic girl.

With so many dead ends on my grandfather's story, I started to consider another possibility: I would never understand his war. Meaning, I would never understand my own.

With no other ideas on what was the right thing to do, I followed the good path that was right in front of me.

D.C. life, bit by bit, won back its turf.

I am done, I said. *Stable, comfortable is good.* Embrace this blessed life. Drink that wine. Get that raise. Open those wedding presents.

GAO made it easier by assigning me to Iraq work. It was breathing space where I could still convince myself and others I had skin in the game in those headlines half a world away. GAO dug and exposed; it raked the numbers and the statistics behind them. It was somewhat like reporting, except we weren't writing about people as much as we were exposing the policy cracks that failed them. It was steady. It fit this new life, so I kept at it. Plus, I wasn't sure if I trusted myself to inhale the vibrancy that was the soldiers' story anymore.

But it was not as easy as I'd hoped it would be. In moments where I did not busy myself with our marriage, the headlines of Iraq crept back in. I thought of my grandfather and his determination not to live as a regular man. I watched my colleagues' bylines as they went into and out of the theater.

I thought of the choices I was making, probably too much. And when I doubted, I just told myself I was overthinking it. I worked to stay lulled in the comfortable and easy, in the late dinners in front of a TV, nights out at bars with my spouse, days filled with my job and online shopping.

It was an internal balancing act that was not going to last. Eventually, all that was tied to the discussion of war, even my search for my grandfather's records, became a tired and divisive theme in our home. They kept me at a distance, and kept my husband from the life he wanted. Truth, I found comfort in that distance and I let those wars build a wall between us.

Winter marked six months of marriage, and they were dark. We fought much harder than a couple in honeymoon bliss should have fought, and hurt each other more than a couple that had just said "I do" should have been able. We were not on a track to have children, we were on a track to divorce. I was not surprised when on my 35th birthday, my husband said he couldn't join me in Texas for a celebration of this milestone. Instead, I boarded a plane for friends in Austin, letting them know there was a happy hour to be had.

As my Southwest flight touched down and taxied to the gate, a text popped up on my phone.

"Would you guys like a ride from the airport?"
It was my high school best friend, offering a ride into town. He was trying to do something nice for my husband and I, since

he'd just skipped our wedding.

I hadn't seen Bill in years. We'd met at church when we were both 15. I walked into my youth group at Dallas' All Saints Catholic Church on a Sunday afternoon in 1989 to discover a mop of blond surfer bangs, a black Don Johnson jacket, a fedora and a new friend. He was a piano player and he was already messing around on some chords. When that teenager saw me walking toward him to say "hi," his blue eyes smiled in a half flirt and half smart-ass look that didn't drop my stare as he started into the first verse of Richard Marx's "Right Here Waiting."

He became my go-to guy for girl-ask-guy high school dances, the voice on the other end of the phone. I was the one who pursued school accomplishments and honors classes like trophies; he was the rebel who actually read the books. Then I got my first serious boyfriend, and Bill became my lifetime *we're just friends*. A connection that had stretched thin at times, through moves to different cities, through his first marriage and through years of losing touch. But every time we reconnected, it was like no time had passed. His was a friendship I was so grateful to have.

"He didn't come," I texted back. "It's just me." The screen went dark.

Then a response.

"Would you like a ride anyway?"

I should have said no, but I didn't.

About a moment after his text popped up, I remembered how happy I'd been to send Bill a wedding invite.

And now he was driving toward the airport, coming to get me. I ducked into the bathroom by baggage check, brushed my hair. Dug for my lipstick and reapplied mascara.

Why? I thought. It was always good to see my old friend, but this nervousness — where did that come from? But I was too anxious. So instead of a gut check I added a stroke of blush.

By the time I got outside to passenger pickup his dark green Volkswagen was pulling up. Our eyes met. *Wow I'd missed him.* We had an awkward happy hug and got down to the business at hand, which for me was namely avoiding any acknowledgment of how glad I was to see him and instead giving him driving directions to my hotel.

As we pulled on to 183 North he was the one to break the silence.

"Congratulations on your wedding," he said. "I'm sorry I missed it."

I remembered getting his email, *"Something's come up ..."*

"You've had quite a year ...." He started again, rattling off some of the milestones he knew about, the wedding, a new house, my work.

I could have just left it there, like I usually did. It was the D.C. way. An image of success, because failure scared people.

But I could never be that way around him. What I knew was that I was hyper alert, scared maybe. I was aware of the individual dials on his dashboard, the light stubble on his face.

What was going on?

"Are you OK?" he asked, then put his eyes back on the road. Since we'd met Bill had been my reality check.

At 17 and pining.

At 22, dead broke but employed.

Now, at a loss for words.

The next time I opened my mouth I wasn't masked by D.C.'s "professional nice" or the layers of the everything that had piled back on since 2003. Those false scabs fell so fast again that by

the time I turned to my best friend and opened my mouth I was
dizzy.

"I'm a mess," I said, glancing sideways with a smile that tried to
convince both of us, even then, *that's OK though, really. I'll figure
this out. I got this.*

Then I spoke once more, in a weak tone because the truth of
my life had been suffocated for years and this was all the energy it
had left to make it to the surface.

"I've made a mess of things."

Then Bill gave me a smile that was compassion and love and the
firm belief that this too would pass. And for the first time in years
I felt like it would.

We arrived at the hotel, Bill dropped me off at the roundabout
driveway of the downtown Residence Inn. I weakly grabbed my
bag, waved him off with instructions on how to meet up later.
Then I went upstairs, where my Texas girlfriend Caryn and a
dreaded phone call home awaited. "Well, have a good time," the
less-than-spirited voice on the other end of the line said.

We were newlyweds. But neither voice on the line registered
enthusiasm. I didn't know why we were trying.

***

A few hours later, surrounded by friends at Paggi House's
wooden deck by Austin's Town Lake, Bill and I were lost in our
own language. I wasn't anything but what I was in that moment
and oxygen returned. I told him about Iraq and the men I'd met
and Kolfage and 70-year-old warplanes. I told him how I'd fallen
short on finishing my grandfather's story. How I'd fallen short
on my own.

He told me about the joy of learning to fly, about how the

sounds of a King Air turboprop crossing Dallas' endless sky gave him redirection in the weeks after his wife left him.

He'd become a pilot.

Caryn looked over concerned. She saw a connection in my eyes that she had not expected to see in her predictable friend. She suggested we head out; I counter-suggested I wasn't ready to go home just yet. I said this with the determined tone that didn't leave room for debate. I'd see her back in our hotel room after the bars closed. And as all loving girlfriends do, she gave me a hug and told me to call. If I wanted to derail my life, there wasn't anything she would do to stop me.

"Why didn't you come to my wedding?" I asked Bill later, or more likely, slurred. *Maybe I wouldn't have made these same choices*, I thought.

"I couldn't watch you walk down the aisle," he said gently. The night went on; a 2 a.m. moment of truth arrived. The good flood of memory and the fit of the present swirled into a violent storm of attraction. Austin's House Wine demanded it, Texas' warm breeze demanded it, a lifetime of friendship demanded it and the hand he was holding already knew it.

"I've always loved you."

I didn't know how true those words were, until they were in front of us.

Shit. I was married, and I shouldn't have been. And my husband should have been married, just not to me.

I kept this hard secret for a couple of months. I stayed married even as I dreamed and texted and emailed the hopes of a life with Bill. My first wedding anniversary approached. I knew I could no longer be married. The way I unmarried was terrible.

Days before our first wedding anniversary, I left my marital home in a manic act of grandstanding, about hypocrisy, about how we both knew things weren't what they should be. Then in a follow-up cruel and explanatory phone call I admitted everything. *Our marriage should be over,* I said. It didn't matter that it was just a kiss, because I realized I was in love, and I no longer belonged there.

And then silence.

Then my husband's cracking voice.

Then the reminders of the years spent dating, of the church vows and shared family Thanksgivings and the faces of a whole chorus of relatives who were worried and disappointed.

I am an awful person. I am right back to who I was in 2003. Erratic. Unmoored. Immoral.

Every day of stability and normalcy gained in the years since, shattered.

Because it was built on nothing true, my grandfather said, as he watched sympathetically from the wings.

My husband's voice on the line was choppy and despairing. What killed me more than anything else: He was concerned. For me.

"Just come home," he said. So I did.

I'm so sorry, I was trying to be this good person. I failed. I will be this, for you.

I'd gotten so far. I was in love. But the second I came into conflict I folded. I'd found just enough strength to finally say "This isn't right."

I didn't have what it took to take the step after that.

I don't deserve to leave, like some visitor who's tired of this conflict. I'm his wife.

I don't know why my husband's response was so shockingly unexpected: *Don't leave.* But once he asked, I lost all remaining strength to go.

"You can never talk to Bill again," he said.

"I won't."

I relayed that promise and my intention to follow it to the man I loved in a voice that was empty and dead inside. Because I was. Three terrible months passed. My husband and I had justified angry fights and tears of regret. We became a more honest, frayed version of the couple we'd committed to. We were still hanging on.

Then it was September and I was headed back to Iraq, as a government auditor this time.

In that Dulles airport goodbye my husband and I were sad and aching, angry and kind. A terrible mix of conflicted emotion that meant we just stared at each other in the final moments at the passenger drop off even as we both hoped for relief.

He drove away, and I began the walk through the reflective tiled floors toward international departures.

I looked up and asked my grandfather: "Was this inevitable?"

Of course it was, he said. *You even wrote about it.*

Tell me you see my hope, and I'll fall in love with you before you finish this sentence.

I landed in Kuwait about 14 hours later, after a United Airlines flight that was now part of a well-oiled transit of Americans back into Baghdad.

For the second leg my GAO bosses and coworkers lined up on a Kuwaiti airbase ramp with dozens of military and contractor personnel. We boarded another C-130 to Baghdad, in broad daylight this time. There were even office desks waiting for us on the other end.

You can always tell the newbies, I thought, as we clambered over the cargo hold's webbed netting. Those guys were the excited ones, the ones who bought a last-minute, overpriced and crappy digital camera in Kuwait to strike a hero pose.

You could tell the repeaters, too. Those were the guys on their third or fourth deployment, who were back from another rest-and-recuperation break at home. Those soldiers would find a corner of the hold to cram a backpack and crash out, faces flushed, mouths open in an exhausted snore.

For the rest of the passengers — the weary and the homesick who scanned their Blackberries for one last loving message before they lost the signal — this flight was just one step in the remaining months of their duty in Iraq. The quicker it passed, the closer they were to home. For those non-plussed passengers, their heads were down, cellphones busy.

I fit in nowhere here. I was no longer interested in the hero pose, and my Blackberry was depressingly empty — a harsh reminder of how full of hope it was just a few months before.

Then a thought: *I'd become the bride in my own damn essay.*
I shut the Blackberry off and closed my eyes. With a shudder and sigh, our heavy C-130 lumbered down the runway toward Iraq.
****

My trip to Baghdad was short this time, the military was on the way out. A villa at the Al Faw Palace I'd walked through after it was first occupied by U.S. troops had become a "distinguished visitor" military hotel. The forces assigned to Iraq in these final months of combat more often looked for ways to fight boredom. So we fished. From a pond filled with carnivorous fish that we pulled out of Saddam Hussein's man-made lake surrounding the palace. We watched videos online of baby ducks who unfortunately fell in to this deep, dangerous palace canal of water. Their last chirps were extinguished by the angry swirl of deadly 4-foot flesh eating fish that struck from below, pulling a puff of white feathers with them.

We'd all become numb, I thought.

There were two Iraqs here, the Iraq paid for by the blood and treasure by U.S. taxpayers, a maze of 20 and 40-foot containers that carried hope and waste, supplies and forgotten equipment ordered by squadrons who'd departed the country long ago. Our job was to understand that mess and try to prevent more.

Then there was the Iraq outside the wire, but we didn't get to see that Iraq anymore.

When I returned to D.C., my marriage felt just as divided. We'd promised to go on, so we did. We were good to each other's families, publicly good to each other. Just like we always had been. But there was a deepening anger from my spouse that did not get better with time, and a growing resentment on my end: *Do you know what I just gave up? So I could be this, with you? You say you want to forgive. But you really, truly do not.*

So on a late Friday night, I was alone again in our guest bedroom, wondering what the next step would be.

My grandfather called out softly at first, I barely heard him. His frayed office box and all my notes on his life were pushed to the back of my closet, hidden. They were too much of a reminder of how much I was like him, too close to home.

Nieta, he whispered.

Granddaughter ... he nudged again.

I stared at my computer screen, unwilling. Surely there was something else.

Come, Tara. Take my hand.

There was nothing else.

So I walked to the closet. I picked up his memoirs one last time and in winter 2009 my grandfather and I started again.

11

Let's Go To War

Original crew #30, 448th Bomb Group.

Morrison Air Field, Florida November, 1943
"Have you heard of my grandfather, Richard C. Harris?" It was such a simple question, one I asked again and

again on Internet forums, on long days spent in the Library of Congress, in book searches and purchases — anything on the Liberator. He was nowhere. Not in expensive leather-bound books I bought from antique book stores, not in the pages of likely bomb group histories I found on the Internet. It was a terrible thing to watch the foundation you needed crumble at your feet.

"Has anyone heard of Greenpants?" I asked a new online resource, a haven of WWII air war experts at ArmyAirForces.com. Just a few months earlier, my grandfather threw "Greenpants" out at me as the name of their destination in England. He cackled at his witty prank. Many late nights of web searches later, all I got were scores of "Old Navy" pop-up ads.

Greenpants was a code name Granddaughter, have fun with that, he twinkled, happy for some payback after so many years stuck in my closet.

I got better at the questions I asked these experts and at what clues I shared. The online forum closed around its target, eager to help me find him. I shared the story of Jimmy Stewart, Sioux City, the formal ball, and crossed my fingers.

Through the process of elimination my bomber community found his likely group number. By the 20th thread of the discussion they had identified his plane. My grandfather was assigned to the 448th Bomb Group, 713th Bomb Squadron, headed to Seething, England.

And?? He taunted. *Let's go to war.*
***

CREW #30 - Aircraft #42-52097
2nd. Lt. Richard C. Harris P 0494504
2nd. Lt. William C. Moore CP 0808576
2nd. Lt. Warren R. Auch N 0687803

1st. Lt. Frank S. Phillips B 02043738
S/Sgt. Robert E. Whiteside E 15070206
Sgt. Paul T. Dempsey R 12135037
S/Sgt. Alfred F. Massey AE 31124673
S/Sgt. Grady W. McLaughlen AR 19175031
S/Sgt. Harry T. Rummel G 37272148
S/Sgt. George J. Schible AG 13155700

Passengers
2nd. Lt. Bruce B. McCleary 0799815
M/Sgt. Francis Berrigan 38089023
S/Sgt. Harley A. Kelley 19138718
Sgt. Mervin Koffman 31161869
***

That November 1943 at Morrison Field, Fla., "Crew 30" of the 448th Bomb Group assembled for England. My grandfather had signed the paperwork to accept responsibility for A/C 42-52097, a new $305,711 Liberator fresh off the assembly line from Ford's Willow Run. Their crates of supplies were organized. Tents. Mosquito netting. Winter clothes.

His crew gave their shiny new bomber nose art and a name, "Lonesome Polecat," because the young men on board were fans of the comic strip Li'l Abner. The Lonesome Polecat was a B-24H, built for a crew of 10, tight with 11; overflowing with their manifest of 14. On the day of their departure, the 18 bladders in the bomber's wings were swollen with fuel. The bomb bays, crevices and seat gaps crammed with baggage and provisions, and extra jump seats latched in for the less-than-comfortable ferry ride.

U.S. bombers were flown to war along two battle routes: The Northern ferry route took planes and crews over Iceland. The route assigned to the 448th was the Southern ferry route, skipping along the South American coast before making an unnerving flight across the Atlantic. On their day of departure, the 14 men approached their aircraft. The walk gave each man just enough time to get a slightly sick feeling: *We were really going.* Across the ramp, 25 other crews of the 448th Bomb Group did the same. It was only about a third the 448th's total bombers. The group was staggering its arrival into three waves because Seething could not absorb all those new airmen and aircraft at once.

On Lonesome Polecat, Dick's engineer, Staff Sgt. Robert Whiteside reached his arm through the gunner's window and felt for the bomb door valve. The aluminum belly snapped open and rolled halfway up, allowing each airman to swing underneath, grab for the narrow catwalk and hoist himself in. A ground mechanic flipped fuel valves 1, 2, 3 and 4 to "on," which opened the gates to a maze of tubing that fed fuel from the rubber bladders in the wings to the engines. The mechanic jumped out, walked around the aircraft and gave each propeller a slow spin to pull the four engines clear of debris or buildup.

Inside, my grandfather adjusted his left seat. His co-pilot sat right. In the cockpit there was a dual set-up and it often took both pilot and co-pilot to apply the force needed to mechanically will the plane true. Two sets of rudders and brake pedals at their feet. Two control wheels. A set of throttles within reach of both men.

The engines closest to the bomber's body started first, one at a time. Lt. Moore looked out the bomber's windows to make sure ground crew were out of the way.

"All clear!" Moore shouted, then reached with his right hand and pumped the fuel booster switch. One ... two... three... four... each push fed a small burst of fuel into engine No. 3, priming it for ignition. He held the switch firm and clicked the No. 3 starter, holding it for 10 seconds before throwing the switch to "Crank." With a rumble and a crack, No. 3 engine fired. The whole of the Liberator began to vibrate. My grandfather ran No. 3 warm through the increasing rates of spin and Moore reached down to start the process again. Engine No. 4 ignited, then No. 2, then No. 1. A ground mechanic stood outside, ready with an extinguisher in case excess fuel pooled around the engines and caught fire.

They were ready. The bombardier pushed the valve to pull the bomb bay doors shut. Dick released the brakes and Lonesome Polecat's 65,000 pounds lurched to motion.

Dick was at the edge of the runway, keeping his heavy aircraft steady. Four propeller-driven engines rocked her forward, the bomber's two tails see-sawed her back. Inside, 10 men in the waist looked at each other. Their faces were flushed with the heat the bomber churned from the Florida asphalt and pushed into their lungs.

My grandfather looked up.

It is time, he said.

Lonesome Polecat was next for take-off, her engines held at 1,000 RPM; wing flaps extended one-fourth. Dick turned the Liberator into the wind and opened the throttle to full. And with the weight of both pilot and co-pilot, I watched my grandfather hold Lonesome Polecat to the line as she gained speed and roared flat into the Florida sky.

****

From Dakar we flew to Marrakesh, that Moroccan capital of vice and dirty sex shows, Arabic women peeping lustfully and invitingly through their veils. We lost one of our ships and crews in the Atlas Mountains near Marrakesh. And then on to Land's End where we lost another ship and crew, this one crashed on landing.

In his memoir my grandfather said his squadron lost men before they ever reached Seething. There were no dates on the crashes, of course. So I dove back into the records to find those flights.

The bombers were departing Marrakesh, ready for their final leg. *So close to war.* Lt. Joseph Shank was 14th in the order for takeoff. He also had a swollen crew of 14 and all the extra cargo and fuel. The tower warned them: After takeoff, circle the field once before pursuing the final westward heading. The planes needed the time to climb to 9,000 feet to safely clear the ominous peaks to the East. Shank took off. It was 11:55 p.m.

At 12:10 a.m. ground crews spotted a ball of fire southeast of the field. Shank's plane failed to respond to radio calls and it took a day to track the wreckage. He and 13 others perished at 7,900 feet when they smashed into the Atlas Mountains. When ground crews finally reached their blackened fuselage, they saw he was only 100 feet from the crest of the ridge.

Twenty-five bombers were left in this first wave of the 448th. They'd been in transit for almost two weeks, camping at bases in South America and Africa. They were on their second to last leg, just one flight away from Seething when they lost another aircraft. In the bad weather and heavy clouds of that leg, the crew of the "Laki-Nuki" unknowingly drifted into German-Occupied France. The pilots thought they were in England so they started their descent. When they cleared the clouds they saw the shocking sight of German aircraft. Pilot Robert Ayrest and Co-Pilot Irwin Litman gunned the engines and raced for the safety of the clouds. Anti-aircraft guns riddled the Laki-Nuki. Their aircraft shook and retched with the tear of each bullet.

Ayrest took the controls and made the English coast, crash-landing the Laki-Nuki on her belly. By miracle all the crew escaped even as the fuselage exploded.

I'd seen this crash before, in a book by another 448th historian, Col. Jeff Brett. As usual my grandfather wasn't in the narrative. "On striking the ground, blue flames engulfed the bomb bay," Brett wrote of the Laki-Nuki's final moments.

I looked back at Dick's words, and I realized he was there. He was watching, irritated, from the cockpit of Lonesome Polecat. "Then on to Land's End, England ... where we lost another ship," he wrote. "This one crashed on landing."

My grandfather closed his eyes. "We had filled the bomb bays with Scotch whisky," he dictated to Abuela. "All of it lost."

You were there, I said to him.

Of course I was, he said back. *It burned bright blue.*

Ayrest and most of his crew died three months later during a Feb. 10, 1944, mission.

Why couldn't you date your missions? Were you afraid? Did you miss these men?

He ignored this.

It was good Scotch too, he said. And then he left to refill his glass.

12

Greenpants

S *eething, England 1943*
Almost as soon as the ArmyAirForces.com community had identified the 448th Bomb Group and Dick's first plane, one of them reached out:

"Have you heard of Patricia Everson?"

Patricia was just nine years old when the 448th Bomb Group arrived in her English farming village. That November 1943 she met her first airman. She was standing outside her schoolhouse with the rest of the town's children, giddy with excitement. It was right before Thanksgiving. She and her classmates had been invited to a holiday party at Seething's new U.S. air base.

Overhead, a half-dozen Liberators were landing at Seething for the first time. "Lonesome Polecat" and my grandfather's crew were among them, directed to make an operational base out of a large, muddy field. The runway wasn't finished; neither was the housing. But in a few weeks these bombers would attack Berlin and much of Germany's industrial base.

A canvas-colored truck rumbled to a stop in front of the gathered schoolchildren. Ground crews from the bomb group's 58th Station Complement Squadron, men who had worked for two months straight to get this base up and running, were happy for the break. They lifted Patricia and her classmates onto the truck bed and drove back to the base.

Patricia was awed. She had never met an American before. In her head she was bold with questions. *Were they like Huck Finn and Tom Sawyer,* from her schoolbooks? When she walked inside the domed, metal building, rows of young airmen cheered at the sight of the kids, so happy to feel a bit of holiday "normal." It scared her quiet. She picked a seat at the end of a long table and only said "yes please," or "no thank you," as her eyes grew wide at foods she'd never seen.

"They put Jell-O on meat! Nobody in this country had ever heard of cranberry sauce before," Patricia said.

After the meal the airmen gave the schoolchildren bags of sweets as gifts; Patricia went home with her questions still tugging.

For the next two years, the 448th's Liberators were her world. Seething's schoolboys loitered on the aircraft hardstand to watch the mechanics work. They snuck through the brush off the edge of the perimeter track to guide rogue airmen without leave passes to the nearest pub, Mundham House Garden. For the fee of a few pieces of candy the kids would stand watch outside the door, rushing in to yell "snowdrops!" when they spotted the approaching telltale white paint of MP helmets.

The kids felt as if the bombers were their own. They could tell a good mission from a terrible one purely by listening.

"I could lay in bed on a cold winter's morning and hear the "putt-putt" that started those four Pratt and Whitney engines," Patricia said. "The noise when they took off was tremendous. They would taxi down the perimeter track — over three miles in length — and take off in 30-second intervals. The noise … you'd think it was never going to take off. The birds wouldn't even sing for a while."

The Americans made life in Seething exciting. Every morning 12-year-old Jim Turner rode his bicycle out to a small road at the edge of the runway to call out to each warbird as it rumbled by. "Little Shepard! Ice Cold Katie! Hello, Natural!" The waist gunners gave a cheerful salute back as they rolled past the kid. *It was nice to be missed.*

There were almost 3,000 men from the 448th Bomb Group at Seething now and 70 of their bombers. The ground crews crammed the aircraft and their maintenance equipment on to all available runway, taxiway and livable space at the airfield and prepared to bomb Germany.

Those early missions were terrible. Their mission sheets almost always recorded loss. On one of Dick's mid-December 1943 flights, of the 26 bombers that took off, 21 made it back.

That was an average day's survival.

When they landed, their glass nose turrets were cracked from attacking fighters. Flak holes riddled their wings and aluminum hulls. Ground crews would swarm the smoking and damaged aircraft. They had ambulances ready for bullet wounds and broken bones; pours of whisky for shattered nerves.

"After the group had flown five missions, and each of us had flown one of them, a statistician flyer worked out the numbers and decided it was statistically impossible for any of us to survive five missions," Dick wrote.

"The condemned men wanted to play. We did our playing in Norwich."

***

Terry was just 200 miles away, in Aldbourne with the 506th Parachute Infantry Regiment, in his new Baker Company. In early spring 1944 he used his leave to surprise his brother. He arrived at Seething in time to see the first bombers returning from that day's mission.

"Somehow Terry learned where I was stationed – classified information," my grandfather wrote, impressed at his little brother's sleuthing.

"He came to visit while I was out on a mission. As planes began to return to Greenpants they were met by ambulances to take the wounded and one or two made crash landings. When the last plane had landed, there was still no brother."

"Did you see Dick Harris?" Terry asked one of the other returning pilots.

"Oh sure," the pilot replied. "The last time I saw Harris he was in flames and going down over France. I'm sorry."

I had been in flames and going down, my grandfather said. *I had an engine fire.*

The fire extinguisher could not put out the fire so he put his bomber in a steep dive. He pushed the airframe until it shook and he beat back the smoke; when he leveled and returned to course he saw they'd been left behind. But he got his bomber back to Seething, crew intact. And when he lowered himself out of the plane, he saw Terry waiting there, grinning on the ramp.

"Terry and I had a great reunion," he said.

The brothers hugged tight, thrilled to share this England experience. *Can you imagine what they must think back home? Terry said to Dick. We were just two kids from Glendale.*

Dick set out to treat Terry like a king. He gathered together his spare officer's uniform and gave him his .45 automatic.

Of course I was able to get another and more ammunition for myself, Dick added, importantly.

The men secured a car and headed the 10 miles to Norwich where my grandfather heard all the details of Sobel that Terry could never put in his letters. How his brother had a plan to redeem himself. He was going to be a Pathfinder. A paratrooper who jumped first.

We are training even harder now, Terry said. *The day is near.* They drank in the car on the way to Norwich, they drank as they strolled the River Wensum, two handsome uniformed Americans eager for company. They drank at the Bell Hotel. They danced at the Samson and Hercules Dance Hall, then danced some more at the American Red Cross Club. They drank as they belted out RAF songs to the pretty barmaid all the men were after at The Vine, and at another pub the airmen always called "Backs" for its owner. They kept drinking as they poured themselves back onto Seething piss drunk after a raucous evening with Norwich's women and its ample public houses.

"The girls were more than willing. They were eager," my

114

grandfather happily reported.

They fell asleep in Seething's Nissen Hut barracks laughing like they did as kids. The next morning, the two grown sons had a friend on base take a portrait of them, then Terry began the journey back. Dick headed to the officers' hut, ready for another day of war in the air.

Come find me, Terry said before departing. *The women are even prettier in Aldbourne.*

When the war ended, even though it meant that her own father was coming home safely from his post in the Royal Air Force, Patricia sat in her window and cried.

"Life just seemed really drab and empty after that," she said. Several years later, she walked back onto the Americans' base. "I went back to the airfield as a teenager to gather wildflowers. The runway was still stretching into the distance. But lots of the buildings had been taken away. Never has anywhere been so empty and desolate. And I thought, 'Well, I am never going to forget you. I am going to try and keep your memories alive.'"

But life has its own plans. Patricia married and built a home in Seething. It seemed like she was always busy when small groups of veterans came to the town to remember.

In 1983, some members of the 448th, joined by a larger group of veterans from the 2nd Air Division, chartered a bus to take them to many of the old English airfields. When the men realized there was no 448th memorial at Seething, they asked whether one could be built either on the airbase, or in a nearby churchyard.

Patricia wasn't impressed at the town's initial response; the parish suggested a small reception.

"'A cup of tea and a bun!' I said, 'Oh no we won't! We've waited a long time for this.'"

But the town had no money, so Patricia and her brother, Reggie, and Jim Turner raised 500 British pounds and planned a huge reunion, inviting all the villagers who had moved away. Patricia could not wait for the party.

Two and a half weeks before the reunion, there was a midnight knock on the door.

Patricia's mother and Reggie, killed in a car crash.

Reggie was supposed to sit next to Patricia to welcome the 448th back with a church service. Instead, she faced two coffins. Two weeks later, in June 1984, the veterans returned.

A lost Patricia got through the 448th's ceremony. But she was still unable to voice the questions in her head.

"Once again I was not emotionally able to ask all these questions, to make the contacts I'd waited so long for," she said.

In the dark weeks that followed Patricia thought about all her brother had wanted to do for the 448th, and now never could. She had to ask the questions.

You only have one life, she told herself. *You have to start making contact.*

"I couldn't type, I hated writing letters and I had no money. But I decided I would start writing to these men and ask them about their memories," she said.

Lt. Leroy Engdahl, one of the 448th's first pilots, helped Patricia track the initial addresses.

Each letter was handwritten, on blue Air Mail sheets. Never more than two pages — the postage would be too much. She asked: "How old were you when you arrived? Were you air crew or ground crew? What did you think of living in Seething? Did you make any friends?"

"It was great therapy to me after losing my mum and brother. Lots of times I wouldn't be able to sleep, so I would sit and write." The first time an envelope arrived with photographs she was nine again – except this time she was skipping around her house in joy. She saved money to make negatives of the prints and posted the originals back.

Word of her effort got out and more letters started flooding in. The stories and connections of the past. By 1987 the town had restored Seething's Control tower as a tribute to the WWII airbase U.S. bombers knew as "Station 146." Seething hosted reunions in 1987, 1990, 1992, 1995 and 1998. The letters grew to volumes of correspondence – more than 50 albums of stories and photographs.

The farm girl who never left Seething became the heart and memory of the 448th. Every summer Patricia carried those albums up to the top of the control tower, to help host it as a museum for visiting schoolchildren and visiting families of the 448th.

And sometimes, when a new family found her, she thought, "I know that name."

But she did not know my grandfather. So Patricia went to work. It did not take long for my email to light up – she'd found 13 of his missions among her files. Patricia did this for no charge, no request for help of her own. She even apologized that she couldn't find more – her records were incomplete.

It was the first real foothold I had on my grandfather's service and my gratitude was deep. Online I saw endless new posts by other families and realized this search for the past – it was not just mine. In forum after forum I read their queries: *Did you know my uncle? Did you know my father? He never talked about the war ...*

The records at the National Archives were supposed to be accessible online years ago. But it was the government, there was always delay. For most of the 448th families it was too expensive to pursue the histories of their fathers and uncles and grandfathers the way I had tracked mine. Even if their own grandfathers had actually recorded the dates they flew, the reports were only available on paper files at the Maryland National Archives campus. It often took more than one try to find a specific mission in the files. Getting the right boxes pulled to search through was a multiple-step process that could take most of the day. I was lucky; I had the luxury of only a 45-minute drive each time I had to try again. For others a search required weeks of vacation time, hotel bills and flights that many families could not afford.

Each weekend I was there, I got a clearer idea of the volume, how it was likely I could look at this endless paperwork and for lack of attention or bad filing, I might miss an important record. Each mission's paperwork took up one or more protected folders. Each folder held pages and pages of missions. Folders were stored by the dozens in gray, hard storage boxes.

There were hundreds of boxes.

For families who didn't live here, I knew they'd never have the same gift I was lucky to have: time.

I turned to my grandfather.

We'll finish this.

I started to respond to requests from 448th families: daughters, sons, grandchildren. Their fathers too had never talked about the war, and now they were gone. The lucky ones had flight logs. Most everyone else just had a few passed-down stories, a photograph and an unfulfilled longing to understand the family they'd lost.

I'd drive over to the Archives after work on Wednesdays, which was the Archives' weeknight late hours until Congress cut its funding. You could ask for 24 boxes at a time; boxes that would fill a whole cart. I'd go over again on Saturday mornings and spend the whole day immersed in the lives and deaths of men 70 years in our past. I gathered their stories one browned mimeographed sheet at a time, under the hot lights of the Archives' photo stands. I developed a system for mass efficiency. Open a box. Open a folder. Pull out a sheet. *Click.* Lay the sheet aside, pull another, *click.* My arms and hands got fast at this rhythm, pausing only when the paperwork was too fragile or I'd let too many hours go and I realized too late I was dizzy with dehydration under the lamps' halogen heat. The Archives' staff began to recognize me, a disheveled girl in a fleece who wore a wedding ring, but was always alone.

1,000 pictures. Then 7,000 pictures. Shot each Saturday, several hundred at a time. 18,000 pictures.

I was obsessed with these records, I felt at home among them. By helping the families of my grandfather's bomb group find their stories I was redefining my own, one sheet at a time.

On one of those days, the text on one of the passing sheets caught my eye. It was the pilot briefing for March 18, 1944.

Each of the 448th's four squadrons were listed at the top of the page.

The 712th was codenamed "Snakebite."
The 714th, "Featherbroom." The 715th, "Spinage."
The 713th Bomb Squadron, 448th Bomb Group: "Greenpants."
"I did a little happy dance in the Archives when I saw that one :)!" I posted online to my friends at ArmyAirForces.com.
See, I was right all along, my grandfather said.
You said it was a code name for your destination, I told him back, rolling my eyes. *That wasn't even close.*

13

An Uneven Spring

448th bombers taxi for takeoff on another mission from Seething, 1944.

Back at Willow Run, Rose ran her hands over the rivets of A/C 42-95075, a new B-24H model: more gunpower. It was January 1944. By now, Willow Run was fast and efficient.

Ninety-four Liberators were on the final 18-day lines at any given time. Willow Run bested even Sorenson's dreams and clocked its fastest time, producing a finished bomber every 55 minutes.

In her time off, Rose watched the hangar doors. She waited for her favorite moment, after a bomber completed the 90-degree pivot on the line and got its final 40 feet of wingspan. She waited to watch it roll outside for the first time, its aluminum fully stretched into the sun.

It was on one of these breaks that Rose saw a young woman her age on the ramp, a white silk pilot scarf fluttering from her neck. A new bomber was primed outside Willow Run's hangar doors, ready. The company tests were complete, it was on track for delivery. Rose's eyes went wide as she watched the woman continue toward the aircraft, swivel under the bomb bay and take the right seat.

"When she saw other female pilots taking the bombers — she knew she wanted to join them," Rose's daughter Vickie Croston told me from Conroe, Texas. To understand how the warbird had changed Rose's life I'd found her surviving daughter, Vickie.

Rose asked her supervisors at Willow Run to let her try out for the program. They said no.

Then she asked again. She desperately wanted to fly. The government's reply: *Not as a single mother. Stay with your little ones.*

So instead, that January 1944 Rose was positioned on the outside the latest aluminum shell to track up to her station, working a row of pre-drilled holes when a manager called her over.

"Rose, I'd like to introduce you to Walter Pidgeon, the actor. He's making a film on war bonds to support the war."

Walter was entranced, stunned. She was even prettier than the poster; brown soft curls tied back in her scarf, sweet eyes and a pretty smile. And she was real.

121

I must have her in my movie, Walter thought. He'd found a real-life "Rosie the Riveter."

The group walked off to the side and a quick business decision was made.

A few months later, the replacement crew of Rose's A/C 42-95075 was preparing for the overseas flight to Seething; this crew was the latest in a constant feed of replacements for the high number of dead or captured crews in England.

The newbies were fresh-faced, packed, ready. Their shiny new bomber had nose art and a name: "Happy Hangover."

A few days before takeoff the men got leave. Relax. Don't think about departure. It was so easy to slip away into the playtime of West Palm Beach, to the sun-kissed hostesses that offered beach parties, surf and admiration. Some made plans with their new hostess friends to meet at Hedley's Bar that evening, others piled into the nearby Palace Theater. The show, as usual, started with a war production newsreel. The men sat up; they knew departure was any day now.

The topic was the same as always, Buy War Bonds. But the setting caught their eye. Willow Run, Mich., was a place they'd never visited. It filled the screen. The camera panned wide over a field of new B-24 Liberators and the billowing smokestacks of Ford's greatest plant. Then, a close-up. First the shine of the aluminum siding of a bomber. Then a pretty brunette took her gun, focused and popped a rivet. The men hooted and cat-called in appreciation. And Rose Leigh was forever sealed into history. "She was at the right place at the right time," her daughter said, as she emailed me photos from the past. The first was a colorized photo I'd seen on the web, in online tributes to "Rosie." Then two I hadn't: Rose under the hood of her car, wrestling the carburetor. Rose balancing on a stone ledge in Michigan, the wind lifting her pleased smile as it blew her hair back.

For Rose, the war opened the door to the life she wanted. But when the war ended, Willow Run told her: Thank you, it is now time for you to go home.

"That didn't sit very well with Mom," Vickie said. "Besides, she couldn't. She still had to support her children."

Instead, Rose moved to Louisville and built airplane engines for Curtiss-Wright. She met an Army soldier stationed at Fort Knox while out rollerskating; remarried, and had Vickie. She went to beauty school, drove a taxi, raised her newborn daughter. She started her own business, Rose Builders, and constructed homes like her father.

Over the years Rose did not fixate on her brush with fame. She didn't own a copy of the film. Vickie never watched it with her mother.

Maybe balancing gains and opportunity with war was difficult for her, too.

But Rose was still not living the life she wanted; her second marriage ended in divorce. In moments alone, 30 years after her time at Willow Run, Rose thought: I still want to fly.

So at age 52, at Kentucky Flying Service, Bowman Field, Rosie the Riveter learned to fly. Once she had her license, Rose took Vickie into the sky with her. She taught her daughter the beauty of these mechanical birds and the art of navigation.

In 1978, Rose couldn't recover from a stall and crashed. She was blinded in one eye and lost a kidney.

"She had to give up her flying dream, which caused her great sadness," Vickie said. As Rose healed, she fell in love a third and last time, and remarried.

Five years after her mother's death, Vickie heard a calling. She took the coursework, passed the check ride.

She is now a commercial pilot in Texas.

"Mom proved it is never too late," Vickie said.

***

Rose's bomber Happy Hangover left Willow Run and departed Florida for Seething as a replacement crew for the 448th, because my grandfather's bomb group was having a terrible spring.

Flying in a Liberator was like driving in a 1970s Ford pickup on a gusty day with the windows down. The entire airplane was open air and heaved left, right, up and down as it pushed through the air. The bombers flew close together, in staggered, diamond-shaped formations to protect themselves against diving German aircraft. But the proximity was also deadly. The unwieldy responses of the big bombers meant that aircraft in formation sometimes collided and fell. Sometimes bomb bay doors for one formation opened too early, hitting other bombers who were flying below. The men in these planes only had a few hundred hours under their belts when they took them into England's clouds with youthful bravery and a prayer that they would get home.

The flying was miserable, too. There was no pressurization, that luxury of modern flying that kept the climate and airflow at levels safe and comfortable for passengers and crew. There was wind and cold. There was no central heat.

Inside the airplane, when the Liberators were on a bombing run, nothing prevented an airman from falling through the open bomb bay doors to his death save a nine-inch catwalk that was unforgiving, and at 22,000 feet over Europe, often slick with ice. The plane was never designed with the men in mind, something that became evident as each mission returned with dead and injured airmen.

Oh my God, the gas, Dick interjected. It only took a few

missions before he stopped eating the early morning English breakfasts of beans and tomatoes. In an unpressurized cabin 20,000 feet up those foods expanded in his stomach and became incredibly painful.

And those waste tubes, he said. At 22,000 feet, the outside temperature was negative 22 degrees Celsius. With the Liberator's open rear windows, the fuselage was a loud, frozen wind tunnel. The men wore suits heated by electric wires, but in the icy cold the wiring could short and leave parts of their bodies stiff with cold. The relief tubes the men had would often freeze over, if a man was desperate enough to try to use it.

Those were the easy failures. Sometimes the radios broke and they flew silent, blind. The mission reports often recorded bombers having to turn back because one of their four superchargers failed. Without functioning superchargers to force thinning air through the Liberator's engines, the heavy bomber could not maintain speed to remain airborne at high altitudes.

At 22,000 feet the air was too thin to breathe, too. There were oxygen tanks on board, but the tanks could run out or freeze. When they did, Dick and his fellow 448th pilots were forced into lower, more dangerous altitudes to survive.

By the time Happy Hangover joined the 448th Bomb Group, of the 65 original crews, only 10 were left. "And none of those 10 had all their original crews," Dick wrote.

Happy Hangover was shot down a month after it arrived, during a mission over Berlin. Four men died in the crash; six were taken prisoner.

Lt. John Masters, of Kerrville, Texas, was one of the six. He had a shell fragment in his neck, and a jawbone fracture from another bullet. A few days later he was taken to a German service command hospital in Berlin, where the attending surgeon noted his final days.

Masters suffered an aneurysm in his neck. Then sepsis set in. Then pneumonia.

The 27-year-old died in Berlin on July 3, 1944.

The replacement crews were always the most vulnerable, Dick said. This was just another day of war. The 448th had already hit rock bottom a few months before.

The day they accidentally bombed Switzerland.

14

The Day We Bombed Switzerland

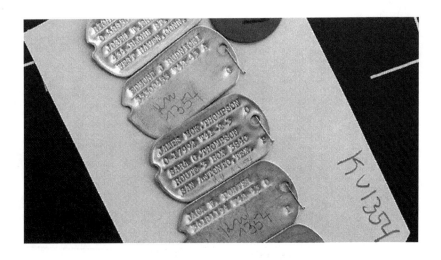

S *eething, England April 1, 1944*

For years, a series of paragraphs in my grandfather's memoirs confused me. The day his "Col. Townsend" was shot down. There were no dates in the paperwork of course, and as it turned out, no "Col. Townsend" either. The whole section was labeled "The Day We Bombed Switzerland."

It was a jarring passage to me. The expectations we had of airpower in Iraq were that pilots would be precise. Airstrikes would be sterile. Angry news stories followed when releasing those bombs meant nearby civilians were sometimes hit too.

When I'd first thought of World War II, I had pictured that air war as an exact and good campaign. I had the false nostalgia of distance and pride. But when the Liberator's aluminum doors opened to the sound of the wind and eight 500-pound bombs rolled out, they were dumb bombs. They hit who they hit. And here was my grandfather, telling me exactly this. Pulling back the curtain.

We hit a whole other country, he said. *It was an accident,* he said.

But it shouldn't have happened …

So we both went back to the stacks, to fill in the missing lines in his memory and show how more than 200 bombers flew over a neutral and important safehaven and struck the citizens below. The day we bombed Switzerland.

It was April 1, 1944. Three hours into that mission, 448th Bomb Group Deputy Lead Navigator Arthur Klein watched the fuel gauge as the numbers on his shaking B-24 Liberator began to flash a warning. If we are going to make it home, we need to turn back now, Klein thought. It was 10 a.m. Klein's crew, my grandfather's crew and almost 200 other U.S. bombers were circling at 19,000 feet above Germany, lost, splintered into several smaller groups and about to accidentally bomb Switzerland.

April 1st started badly and ended worse. Takeoff was scheduled for 6:30 a.m., for a massive strike against the chemical factories in Ludwigshaven, Germany. Which meant the pilots and crews of the 20th, 14th and 2nd Wings were pushed from bed at 3:30 a.m. for coffee and mission briefings.

The 448th's commander, Col. James Thompson, assigned himself as command pilot— the bomber tasked with guiding the entire group to target. But Thompson wasn't rated to fly the bomber left seat in combat. Instead he and the group's officers crowded aboard another already full bomber to guide the mission from there.

My grandfather and his crew were in A/C 41-28602, "Commando." As usual, several of the Liberators had mechanical issues that pulled them out of line. This time Dick's bomber was one of them, his magneto was off. As the Liberators in front of him launched my grandfather taxied back to the flight line for a quick fix.

For the next 30 minutes, the first of the bombers that launched carved a wide circle overhead, as they waited for the full formation to assemble in the sky. Like most days, England's shapeless clouds formed a gray wall blocking the ground below from the sun above. Or a "10/10 undercast," as the men would record it. The bombers easily got separated.

Dick finally got off the ground, 30 minutes later than expected and flew full throttle to catch up with his group. He didn't have to go far; the group was still over England. They spent the time climbing, circling and descending through levels of high haze and undercast to locate the rest of the mission set — scores of additional bombers from the 446th and 93rd Bomb Groups. The formation lost the 446th almost as soon as they found it; the 446th's station at Bungay recalled its bombers after too many aircraft radioed in: *We're lost.*

"No combat wing formation whatsoever," a 446th command

pilot griped at the sight of the disorganized aircraft to his right. The group finally left the English Coast and headed toward occupied France. Thompson reported in: their radio navigation systems were down. Klein reported his were malfunctioning as well. More bad news, Klein determined that their compass was off by 50-60 degrees.

They were hundreds of miles off course.

The bombers climbed again to reorient themselves. But at their weight and higher altitude they burned through fuel even faster. Klein couldn't get a good read on their location. They were supposed to be at the target by now: Ludwigshaven, Germany, precisely at 10:08 a.m.

They didn't know how far off they were.

At 10:02 a.m. Klein called out to the lead: "It is time to get back to base." The aircraft would soon reach a point where they would not have enough fuel to make it home.

Thompson would not accept his navigator's advice. Not when they were over German territory. He signaled through flares that the group would open its bomb bay doors and press on. For another 55 minutes they hunted for the target. There was a continuous relay over the radio: "Bombs away! Bombs away!" No one heeded. Crews suspected it was German interference. But there was no way to be sure and it made a difficult mission even harder.

"There is so much chattering on the VHF!" 44th pilot Lt. Jack Thames scolded.

"We performed several maneuvers to determine our exact location, and burned through more precious fuel," Dick wrote. Thompson "radioed instructions to the other groups to break formation and seek out 'targets of opportunity' railroad yards, whatever."

Klein was hunting, they needed to get rid of their bomb load—and all other extra weight fast — to lighten the ships and get home. By dead reckoning he notified the group they were over Stuttgart, Germany. The operations officer ordered a run.

Commander Thompson dropped his bombs at 11:04 a.m. and the rest of the group followed. One by one they released on the lead.

Dick followed his commander. He reported the bombs dropped "SW of Ludwigshaven, Germany, buildings on both sides of the river."

Pilot 1st Lt. D.E. Sayler watched Thompson's run with disbelief. As each bomber released on the lead, he ordered his own bombardier to hold.

"We did not drop on lead. Thought he was dropping on Switzerland," Sayler reported. He ordered his crew to find an alternate target instead and released his bombs. But even as he reported the strike, he was uncertain.

"Target?" His interrogators asked after Sayler landed. All he could respond back was: "Germany????"

20,000 feet below these lost aircraft, it was a Saturday — Market Day — in Schaffhausen, Switzerland. At 11 a.m. the buildings and streets were filled with commerce and daily interchanges.

The sound of bombers high overhead was not immediately concerning; the town had become used to errant warplanes off course and Swiss fighters regularly chased them off. But this noise ... was different. There were waves of them. By the time the townspeople started to run for cover it was too late.

The bombing run took less than a minute. An estimated 50 Liberators off course dropped more than 400 bombs onto Schaffhausen. Buildings on both sides of the river crumbled in smoke. Forty people were killed walking in the streets and trapped in fires that raged in their stores and homes. More than 270 men, women and children were badly injured.

Was this intentional? The question haunted the rest of the war. Above them, the pilots were unaware they'd just murdered dozens of civilians and jeopardized the relations of an important safe haven. Instead, as they released, those crews fixated on something else: We aren't going to make it home. The aircraft cut speed and altitude in a silent prayer to maximize fuel as they turned toward the border to escape. It made them sitting ducks for German fighters, and the first Liberators to take off that morning were the worst off.

"As each group turned back toward the French border planes started slowing down to conserve gas," Dick wrote. "It became evident that several of the aircraft did not have enough fuel to make it back to England. Our group turned toward the French border where the pilots of the doomed aircraft would order their crews to bail out, and then try to safely crash the bombers alone – with the hope that the French Underground would provide rescue."

At 12:50 448th Bomb Group pilot Lt. Harrison C. Mellor, in A/C 42-110087, dropped behind formation. He'd feathered engine No. 4 on the hopes of stretching the little gas he had left and drift to friendly territory. Top turret gunner William Warren and Radio Operator Francis Marx studied the gas gauges and knew better. This ship was not making it back to England.

Ten minutes later Mellor lost two additional engines. The plane had five minutes of fuel on its remaining propeller. The last to see Mellor's plane was Lt. Kronheim. The pilot looked out the cockpit of his own struggling bomber and saw Mellor drift down. At 13:13 Kronheim reported: Mellor's B-24 was "lost in the soup."

In their final minutes on the aircraft, Mellor and co-pilot Lt. Doug Eames held the bomber in a controlled descent as Marx and Warren secured the ship and their parachutes.

"We were together the remaining 15 minutes destroying equipment and preparing to jump," Marx said. Each of the crew bailed out a different emergency exit. The tail gunner, two waist gunners and the turret gunner pushed through the camera hatch. The bombardier and navigator jumped out through the nose wheel.

Marx, Warren, Mellor and Co-pilot Douglas Eames gathered at the bomb bay doors. But something was off: Warren was hesitating. There was no time. Warren knew the pilot and co-pilot wouldn't jump until he and Marx were out.

Co-pilot Eames noticed that Warren looked nervous. "He was reluctant to jump," Eames told investigators later. But Marx did not notice in time. Marx was only focused on Warren's foot placement so he could copy the movement exactly the very next minute. He did not notice the nerves; just that his friend was taking too long. Then Warren pushed off and slipped through the opening; Marx watched his friend's fall in horror.

"He jumped at an altitude of 9,500 feet. And I watched him fall, until his body could no longer be seen. His parachute had not opened."

Marx, Mellor and Eames followed. Everyone except Warren survived.

He must've gotten injured right before the jump, or in the air, bombardier Marvin Goff thought. Warren "was not the type of man to be too startled or nervous to get out safely."

Two Frenchmen reported that Germans found Warren's body and collected his dog tags. Warren's chute was beside him, unopened.

A casualty officer processed the paperwork on Warren's death and interviewed the crew. They chewed over those final moments, looking for an answer. Marx just knew.

"Any explanation of his fate based in part or wholly on supposition?" his interrogator asked.

"Probably a faulty chute!" Marx replied, anguished. "Probably delayed his jump — discovered too late to be able to dig it out." He remembered the final moments of his friend's life, as he, Mellor and Eames crowded the bomb bay doors. They were losing critical time. They needed Warren to jump. In seconds it would be too late to safely escape.

And Warren knew it. Marx thought. *He jumped for me.*

Now Marx understood why moments before dying, Warren turned to his friend. "With one last handshake and a wave, he left," Marx said.

Thompson's command was over. He watched as the bombers to his right and left fell off formation. Almost everyone else was reporting over the radio they didn't have enough gas to make it to England.

Then Thompson's bomber was hit. The commander gripped his seat as the aircraft gave a low creak and shudder and started to dive. The tail gunner was wounded in the head; the rear waist gunner was bleeding at his right arm, legs and head.

Three P-47s escorting the group rallied around Thompson to protect him. The pilot, Lt. Teague, stayed at the controls and ordered the crew out.

"I'll stay with the plane!" Teague said. "I'll belly-land her!" Thompson turned to look at his pilot. The group commander would not stay with his plane. Thompson headed for the bomb bay doors and jumped.

But Thompson had jumped too late. With only 400 feet between him and the Earth his body slammed into the ground with his parachute still closed.

My grandfather's 713th squadron was gone. When I looked back at the assembly sheet for that day, one by one the squadron aircraft in his formation ran out of gas. 713th Lt. C.C. Knorr was directly in front of Dick, in A/C 42-52098. At 13:00 Knorr fell from formation. 713th Lt. Mellor crashed at 13:10. 713th Lt. Weaver was two ships to my grandfather's right in A/C 42-100109. He went down at 13:25.

"I ordered the remaining pilots to rally around me and we continued," my grandfather wrote. "By the time we reached the French coast there were only three of us left. One went down in the English Channel and one made an emergency landing at the point where we touched the English coastline, just below the white chalk cliffs of Dover."

My grandfather's late takeoff had saved him and his crew. He returned to base with an hour of fuel left. "But when I landed I found half the brass of London waiting," he said. "Switzerland had warned them of the bombing some three hours earlier. I underwent a very stiff interrogation."

Dick didn't write more. He left no clues as to how this terrible day affected him, knowing he'd bombed innocents. What it felt like to be one of the few to make it back. He didn't share how he spent that night, alone, when the officers' tent was empty.

I kept pushing in the paperwork, hoping to find a report where he said something more. So I was back in the National Archives, digging away at April 1, 1944, when I found yet another grayed box.

But there were no mission reports inside. Instead I found rows of dog tags clipped and stored of many of the dead and captured from that failed flight:

Brady. Rudnicki. Porter. Vaughn. Knorr. Padilla. Campbell. Agee. Sarna. Eatherly. Perry. Weaver. Wood. Rice. Byers. Dickey. Tucker. Tipton. Warren. Knowles, Teague.

And their commander, Thompson.

15

Second Chances

Wedding day, Arizona.

Walter Reed's elevator doors opened for Kolfage and he wheeled into a fast hello. He said "hi" to the nurses and to his fellow patients.

He joked and taunted and smiled, to the point that it made the nurses nervous. A steady stream of well-intended evaluations ensued: *It's OK to be angry. You've lost a lot. It's OK to be depressed.* Kolfage ignored them. *They don't know me at all,* he thought. *I'm not depressed. I'm bored as hell.*

He had been at Walter Reed for almost 10 months. He'd faced 16 surgeries. The doctors cut into his remaining piece of arm and both leg pieces, rounding them out, getting them in the best position for a life with prosthetic limbs.

He'd healed, but Kolfage hadn't made much progress in physical therapy. That wasn't completely on him. Walter Reed hadn't anticipated triple amputees, although they had several now. Neither hospital nor patient had known what to expect, and the seams on both had frayed.

Kolfage's parents and girlfriend had arrived at Walter Reed in September 2004, even before Kolfage came out of the medically induced coma the doctors had put him in. The staff weaned him off it slowly, just enough so that he could mumble and start to understand the voices he heard around him.

He knew his family was stressed, that they were thinking: *Holy crap what is his life going to be like?*

By week three of consciousness Kolfage was upright in bed. His arms and legs were still bandaged and seeping but his personality had come back in force. He wanted out of this hospital bed and was hungry for real food. Pizza.

Kolfage's voice was deep and assertive. When you heard it on the other end of a phone call it conjured visions of a tall and willful young man. He was that guy before the attack, he wasn't going to stop being that guy just because he got hit.

He'd been in Walter Reed only about a month before he lowered himself into a wheelchair to get out of there. He was a 21-year-old who wanted pizza, and the hospital staff would just have to deal with it.

He picked up his cell phone and called one in.

Then he pushed himself out of his room, down the elevator and out of the hospital's front doors. He didn't ask permission and he didn't say where he was going. Who was going to stop him?

"I was really medicated at the time," he said.

The old Walter Reed was in a hyper-busy but not entirely safe part of town. The complex itself was set way back on a long lawn. The delivery point was a good football field's distance away, protected by spiked iron gates.

It was the first time Kolfage could really feel the outdoor sun, although it was colder now; October. He rolled and pushed and got to the gate to meet his delivery guy for a pizza.

He doesn't really remember the process of getting the pizza box from the delivery guy, or how the guy reacted, or even paying.

He remembered he could feel the wind on his face. Not that it was great, or refreshing. Georgia Avenue was a heavy transit passage for firetrucks and honking taxicabs. But it was still his. He'd made this meal happen and it was going to start being that way from then on.

Two months in, he started the process to stand again.

Medical staff strapped him to a rotating bed that slowly tilted upright.

"It stood me up," he said.

It was awkward. It was the first time he'd seen the world like this since he'd lost his legs.

Walter Reed's prosthetics were just developing too. The nurses did their best. A prosthetic leg needs to fit the individual bumps and bones of each wounded person it helps, and the hospital struggled in those early days with a quickly overwhelmed crew as more and more amputees arrived at their door. They didn't have enough time or resources to get all the tweaks on Kolfage's new legs.

"It was pretty painful," he said. "It was this hard plastic, it felt foreign to me. I couldn't really stand or put a lot of weight on them."

With each trial the staff would measure and evaluate where the prosthetics did not fit, and send them for adjustment.

"Weeks would go by with no progress getting made, so I would just go back to my room and wait or sleep or whatever," Kolfage said.

Lots of people wondered when Kolfage would hit his wall, when he would feel sorry for himself. Whether he would have his "moment" to decide to not let these grave injuries defeat him. But Kolfage never felt defeated, so he never needed a "moment." He hadn't been one of those warriors who'd been on regular IED-shattered patrols to the point that PTSD trapped him like it did so many others. He'd barely been back in Iraq a few weeks before he walked toward the gym tent and his life changed forever. One moment he was walking; the next moment he was not. Somehow his healthy, flexible young mind had made that transition in a flash; he needed others to as well.

When he wheeled around Walter Reed's hallways, sometimes he looked into the rooms of soldiers with massive head injuries, men who would not get the same chance he had to make it back. It just motivated him further. He was one of the lucky ones.

"I still had my head and I could still function," he said. Kolfage and his wife moved to Fisher House, where they could have more privacy and a setting that felt more like home.

He could already see the limitations of Walter Reed. The hospital's estimated time frame for his healing — for a man who was as grievously injured as Kolfage — was two years.

Hell no, Kolfage said. He wanted a beer and some fun. Anything but the bureaucratic gray labyrinth of military medicine.

He did his physical therapy and got trial legs, the stubbies. Kolfage graduated to a second pair. But they fit terribly. Annoyed, he stuck to his wheelchair. He got an arm and cracked up as it snapped and flew off. He showed me how in occupational therapy, nurses taught him how to pick up a paint brush using his prosthetic hand. The idiot I was, I thought happily, *oh good, they're teaching him to paint.*

Thankfully neither Walter Reed's bureaucracy nor D.C.'s cold could stop this kid. Instead Kolfage frosted the tips of his hair and demanded to go tanning in a huge "fuck you" to that cold February 2005. By spring he was gaming his future in his head. Ten months after he was injured, he told the hospital: I'm leaving. He'd had it with wasting his youth in a dreary building that never quite figured out what to make of him.

But where to next? There was only one answer to D.C.'s winter. Kolfage wanted a place with endless sun. He grabbed his new wife and told an entire community that wondered how he'd make it without them: "I'm moving to Arizona."

When he arrived in Arizona, a grateful Air Force told Kolfage he could have any desk job he wanted. His life was a blank canvas. They got him a wheelchair-equipped van, because Kolfage still wasn't using his legs, and he and his wife tried for regular life. He took his first metaphorical steps back into the "public" world– the non-military world. It was a world he'd been avoiding because of that whole "holy shit" factor when people reacted to his injuries. He started slowly, at Pima Junior College, with a few classes. Everyone breathed a sigh of relief when it looked like Kolfage and his wife found a life with some semblance of normalcy.

Except that's not the way it worked, it never was.

When the pair married beside Kolfage's bed in late 2004, they stared down a wall of the unknown and decided to fight it together. When they divorced in 2008, it was not the unknowns that took them. Once both were given a chance at normal life, they realized this partnership was forged in error. It became bitter, resentful, the end of a young couple frayed by the journey neither bargained for.

After she left, Kolfage sat alone at the kitchen table in his Arizona home. He stared at a pen on the table and asked himself, Can I really do this?

He wasn't thinking about bachelor life, or living alone. He could do that. Could he teach himself to write again?

Kolfage was right handed. A 107 mm rocket shell took that hand to the forearm. He knew what he wanted: to get into the University of Arizona's competitive architecture program. The program only took the top 50 applicants. He put the pen in his left hand. "I couldn't even write my name," Kolfage said. "I had to learn to draw."

Every night for six months, he did just that. He drew. Competitive assignments that took the other applicants just a few hours took him all week. As his drawings started to take shape, he had another thought: "I'm 23. I don't want to be driving a damn minivan." Kolfage enrolled in a program in Arizona to get new legs. He learned to walk again. It was the only way out of that stupid, old person's car. In 2008, he traded the minivan for a black Range Rover, and the University ofArizona sent him an acceptance letter. Of the 50 students accepted, Kolfage was in the top five.

He was ready, too, for other chapters to begin. Namely, girls. Kolfage first saw Ashley years before he was ever hurt. He had just been assigned to San Angelo. He was a cocky kid who saw a stunner working at Chili's, and he proceeded to be an ass when she refused to give him her number. I'm going to marry that girl, he boasted to his buddies.

They became friends instead and hung out in a mutual circle. San Angelo, even with its university and air base was still a small Texas town.

When he was gravely injured and later married she knew, just like the whole town knew. And when he divorced she knew that too. It's just the way small Texas worked.

When he found her on Facebook, he was in the first year of his architecture degree and she was just about to graduate from Angelo State. This time, he got her number.

"And we talked every day," he said. For three months.
"When you click, you click," he said. "She had a really happy-go-lucky personality like mine. We just kind of jived."

The first time Ashley went to Tucson to see him, he wasn't nervous about what she'd think. He felt a good kind of nervousness. A feeling he hadn't had in a long time. Even though she was going to meet a very different man.

"The last time I saw her was before I got injured, obviously," he said.

He pulled up to arrivals at Tucson International Airport in his black Range Rover. He wasn't wearing his legs and Ashley stood there with her small bag. He popped the door and she jumped in.

He always drove without his legs, it was easier. But the kid in him too, he did it to be funny.

"A little icebreaker," he said laughing, and kissed her.

They went back to his place, hung out with his friends and went for beers at a sports bar by the university.

She's so hot, he thought. He pursued her like he tried to at Chili's that night, except this time she was ready, and liked the chase.

That night he got her undressed and he was undressed and his prosthetics were off because man those things were not good in bed. He saw she was nervous. He looked at her with intense blue eyes and the erection of a 24-year-old.

It'll be good, he swore. He gave her a broad smile. *Legs just get in the way.*

Two years later, they were parked at an overlook in Tuscon. They'd moved in together but hadn't rushed marriage. They wanted to date.

But they knew, and on this night Kolfage proposed.

He'd wanted an airplane to fly over, a skywriter so everyone to see his proposal.

"I thought about a cool way to do it for so long, and the airplane was cool, but I didn't have that kind of money," he said.

Instead, he had a glass bottle made and put a key inside. Tied to the key was a note.

"Key to my heart ... I was whipping out all the moves," he grinned.

At sunset, the next chapter of their life began.

16

A Triangle and an Upside-Down T

L ecce, Italy 1944
 After his final mission of his first tour in England, Dick
 wanted to keep fighting. He did not want keep fighting
from cold, wet Seething.

Naturally my grandfather did not bother to mention in his
memoirs which unit he went to next, just that he was headed to
Italy. But he had left me the photograph.

In the Kodachrome print, his bomber's tail was marked with a triangle and an upside-down T. Even though he hadn't remembered his group number, I knew enough about those warbirds by then to know I could track him through the tail.

As air victories in North Africa and Italy increased, the U.S. reorganized its bombers to maximize the gains. After the reorganization, odds were that a pilot flying a heavy bomber in Italy in 1944 was in the 15th Air Force. If he was in the 15th Air Force in a B-24 marked with a triangle and an upside-down T, odds were he was with the 98th Bomb Group, based in Lecce, Italy. The group affectionately known as "the Pyramidiers."

That's where Dick went after England, because his best childhood friend Bill Sawyer was commander of the 98th's 343rd Bomb Squadron. If Dick had to fly bombers, he was going to fly with the guy who'd always been his second in fist fights. Except this time Dick was now Maj. Bill Sawyer's second, his air operations officer for the squadron.

It was warmer there, my grandfather said. And the women.

Once I had the 98th nailed down, I reached out to its historian, a 98th grounds crewman named Herb Harper. Herb had served with the group just a few years after my grandfather left, but with B-29s over Korea. When his war was over too, he started reaching out to the men of the Bomb Group's past. He ended up the Bomb Group's memory, the keeper of their wars.

Herb did what he could to help. But he was old now and he could not travel much anymore. He apologized, there were so many records he lacked.

I didn't even have to look at my grandfather this time.

"I can photograph them," I told Herb. "We'll make the 98th complete."

It's safe to say Dick loved serving in Italy. The things that made his memoirs about this base had very little to do with war. Learning Italian. Sneaking off into the woods with any one of the local families' daughters, who hoped this now captain would take their child back to America. The effort the enlisted men of the 98th put into making their own moonshine, which Dick and the other officers named "Tiger Piss" - until a visiting general took a sip, spat it out and ordered the drink be watered down.

"Change the sign too," the general ordered. "Because visiting USO girls might see it."

The men obliged. They added powdered milk and renamed it "Butterfly Wee-Wee."

With this group Dick made a supply run to Egypt and rode a camel at the Pyramids. Then he decided to ride the camel back to his hotel and figure out a way to load the beast onto his bomber.

That didn't work, but the next time he visited, his hotel and others had a sign: "Absolutely no camels allowed!"

For Dick, according to the stories he left behind, Italy was nights of the men stacking up all the furniture in the officers' club. They would dip their feet in ink, so the white ceilings would bear their crazed foot trails. It was many nights of women. Sometimes the men would try and find a girl to dance naked for them on the officers' club bar. Sometimes it was women he would meet in town, or the women he would meet on leave.

But in the history books it was much, much more than that and I was frustrated not to see it there.

From the history books, the 98th Bomb Group was beloved for its sweet fascination with Snow White and all Seven Dwarfs. Hand-painted images of "Dopey," Bashful," "Sneezy," "The Witch" and the rest graced their bombers' nose art. But the 98th was also infamous for suffering the worst single mission loss in the history of U.S. air war: "Operation Tidal Wave" against Ploesti. Ploesti was a series of refineries in southern Romania that supplied more than a third of Hitler's oil. That target was dangerously defended by a ring of 250 heavy flak guns and cloaked in black, belching smoke. When U.S. aircrews reached Ploesti, Liberators broke in half as ground fire hit their oxygen tanks. They smashed into hidden smokestacks. They were strafed by German ME 109 fighters and eviscerated nose to tail as they flew into taut cables suspended by balloons that sliced through the bombers' formations to shear off engines and wings. On Aug. 1, 1943, the 98th Bomb Group lost more than half of its crews and airplanes during what was supposed to be a surprise attack. They practiced that mission for months out of their headquarters in North Africa, learning to fly 200 mph just 100 feet above their desert tents, so they wouldn't be spotted during their fast and dangerous approach. The formations would rise at last minute another 100 feet to make their run, drop hundreds of bombs and set the refineries on fire.

But the mission was compromised. The Nazis were waiting for them amid Ploesti's smoke. The Archives holds the memory of this day: pages of lost 98th crew names scroll single spaced for entire bombers that were reported missing in action or shot down: 18 pilots. 19 First Officers. 19 Navigators. 19 Bombardiers. 19 Engineer-Gunners. 16 Radio Operators. 20 Turret Gunners. 54 Aerial Gunners. A Combat Cameraman. All lost in the matter of a few hours.

Worse, on August 2, 1943, Ploesti was still standing. In a few weeks it resumed full operations.

For Herb, this was the mission the historians would ask him the most often about. It was the mission that generated all the books. I already knew my grandfather was not in the air with them August 1, 1943. Dick was probably still in Sioux City.

But just as he did in his chapters on the 448th, my grandfather left me no 98th actual missions or dates. So we set back out to the Archives, with the final chapter of his war in our sights.

June 6, 1944

*R*AF North Witham, England and Lecce, Italy. D-Day.

Terry smiled from a back row of paratroopers three rows deep as their photographer cajoled him and 22 other men into looking up for their official combat portrait. It was not an easy task. The men had much on their minds. They had their backs to the sun and their brand-new C-47 Skytrain transport aircraft. It was 6 p.m., June 5, 1944.

A lot of the men didn't smile. Terry had the Cheshire-cat grin of a man who'd got his girl, who'd just won the lottery — not of a man who was about to jump into gunfire over France. To Terry, this moment was just as good. No, it was better. My great-uncle was a 23-year-old on a victory lap. He had his pipe, a gift from his father. He put it to his lips, just as he did in every war photograph we had of him.

When Terry was ripped from Easy Company for standing up to Sobel he feared it would keep him from the war and make him go home a disappointment instead of a hero. The 506th had transferred him to Baker company, then gave him another option: Be a Pathfinder. Terry seized it. Not every man was as grateful to be here, but they were drilled and hardened and were ready. Now this photographer and the load-in were the final things separating these 20-year-olds from the action.

There were more than 300 Pathfinders — men assembled, volunteered or forced with no other options to be part of this mission. Of all the aircraft about to launch over France, the Pathfinders would go first. They would jump gripping holophane lights and Eureka radio beacons — theater-stage like lighting systems the men would assemble into "T" shaped targets on the ground. They would fire up the Eureka to squawk a radio signal to classified receivers on the C-47s behind them; the holophane "Ts" would light up the landing zones for the waves of 14,000 paratroopers to come.

The Pathfinders would take off an hour ahead of the main wave. They would jump in the middle of the night in total darkness. They would jump above tracer fire and razor line to crawl in flooded fields to set up the beacons and guide the way for the rest. War planners considered the Pathfinders' role vital, but

likely a one-way mission. Many of the men considered it suicide.
Terry thought of it as destiny.

He looked directly at the camera and smiled the grin of a man
who was framing for his family how he wanted to be remembered.
It was his last photograph. Proud. Fearless. Happy. He smiled
for little sister Annette, six years his junior, who all the guys had
endlessly teased him about. He smiled for his Easy Company
brothers, who would be dropping on the landing zone he would
set and protect. He smiled for his brother Dick. Did he know
today was the day?

But mostly he smiled for his father.

You can be proud of me now.

Just a half hour before, the gates of the barbed-wire tent city
that had held these crews in seclusion over the past nine days
had opened. Nine days of no phone calls, no outside contact.
The food was good; the games of poker had gotten old. They'd
used the time to sharpen their trench knives, write letters that
would not be mailed ... not yet. The blackout wasn't surprising;
they'd done the same on practice jumps over England. *So maybe
this was just another drill* But the tempo, tension and duration
were

different. Every man had his weapon checked, then re-checked.
On June 1 they got their regular cash payday — but the money
was French. *This was new.* Anticipation flooded into nervousness. It
was Normandy. *Operation Neptune,* they were told. *This is it.*

Briefings got more detailed and each crew was drilled on maps
of specific fields and routes and hedgerows of the landing zones
they would drop into. *Know the fields,* they were told. They were
warned of the guns and defenses Allied spotters had marked.
Watch for the hedgerows. Those natural barriers were borders
of heavy brush or trees in between fields that the French loved

but could hide guns and snipers. The shrubbery made forward movement like a deadly slow track meet with hurdles.

They got new uniforms. Every man who would make this jump on D-Day got his shoulder patch, a black shield with a bald eagle and the yellow-lettered arch: AIRBORNE. But these men also got a second, secret patch they were forbidden to display: a gold winged torch. They were the Pathfinders. The men who would light the way.

On June 3, each of their C-47s got their invasion stripes — three blazingly white and two black stripes that were two feet wide, so U.S. warships off the French coast wouldn't shoot as waves of transport aircraft flew 700 feet above them at 150 miles per hour and only 100 feet apart.

For the afternoon briefing of June 5, 1944 the crews were told to arrive fully kitted. As soon as the Nissen hut doors were shut, they were told the time of departure. From the briefing they went directly to pick up their parachutes. The men held them in their arms as they walked onto the flight line, where a row of smartly-lined C-47s waited. Each of the first 20 aircraft that carried this first wave of 300 men into France were marked with large chalked numbers by each jump door. The planes were numbered to help crews gather at the right aircraft, they also marked the order in which they would drop into combat.

Terry was in Plane 5.

***

1,500 of miles southeast, my grandfather was also in pre-mission preparations. It was 3:30 a.m. June 6, 1944. Dick was drinking his second cup of strong coffee in a briefing room in southern Italy as the pilots of the 98th Bomb Group's 343rd, 415th, 345th and 344th squadrons received a final briefing on what new traps, heavy guns or smoke screens the Germans had erected since their last fateful mission. At 5:15 a.m. their aircraft departed Italy's seductive coast and crossed the Adriatic Sea to Romania. They were striking Hitler too – but not in Normandy. They were going back to Ploesti.

Since that first ill-fated mission against Ploesti, the 98th had regrouped and added replacement crews. The command waited until its replacement pilots were more seasoned; ready. They would take Ploesti down. The operation to do so began that spring.

From April 1944 to August 19th, 1944, when Ploesti finally fell, the 98th and the other heavy bombardment groups of the 15th and Royal Air Forces relentlessly attacked. In those five months, the groups dropped more than 13,000 tons of bombs. An estimated 60,000 airmen flew over Ploesti's smoke-obscured oil tanks. Every mission ended with another man or crew killed, captured or missing in action. In those five months of attacks more than 200 bombers and 50 fighter escorts were lost, and more than 2,000 airmen were killed or missing.

For my grandfather, "Italy was a gentleman's war, except when we hit that dreaded target Ploesti." Ploesti was the target they drank to forget; and in his memoir stack my grandfather also left me the stories of the fear:

"My assistant operations officer — after ten missions or so — became physically ill. By the time we had reached an altitude of ten thousand feet his stomach would be so painfully distended with fear-caused flatulence that he would have to abort the mission. This happened so frequently I had to ground him."

"That was a physical illness, but in the case of one of my bombardiers it was a mental illness. He would perform his job satisfactorily to and over target, drop his bombs, and then, en route back, with the long gradual descent over the Adriatic he would develop hallucinations. He would imagine seeing enemy fighters who would attack and shoot down our bombers. He reported parachutes, then life rafts, and men floating in life jackets. Even with a couple of slugs of whisky in him, his post-mission debriefings were wildly imaginative."

"There was another case of a pilot who suddenly refused to fly any more combat missions. Instead of court-martialling him, I sent him to Bari [15th Air Force headquarters] for a mental and physical evaluation. He returned a few evenings later to find a group of us gathered at the bar. When I asked him how it had gone he produced orders transferring him from combat status to Air Transport Command. We all congratulated him, and truly meant it. He finished the drink I bought him, went across the street to his tent, and blew his brains out with a .45 automatic. He was afraid of combat but not of taking his own life."

On the morning of June 6, 1944, the 98th set out to strike Ploesti again.

***

Terry's base at RAF North Witham still had the last wisps of sunlight when the first C-47, "Neptune 1" of the Normandy D-Day invasion turned its nose to the runway. It took off at 9:54 p.m., June 5, 1944 and launched "the tactical beginning of the liberation of Europe."

The transport was followed by Neptunes 2 and 3. They formed over England in "V" flying shapes of groups of three, like geese circling overhead as the rest of the 20 aircraft took off and built their attack formation in the sky.

At 11:02 p.m. Neptune 5 took off. Terry and 22 others who made up this crew were inside. He'd buckled his trim 160-pound body into the metal bench seating that lined either side of the aircraft. His arms and shoulders touched the men on his left and right, and their knees were forward, just 10 inches from the knees of the men facing them, benched in on the other side. They were a darkened, seat-belted mountain of camouflage equipment and uniforms broken up only by the whites of their eyes and teeth.

Terry's back was pressed against the outer frame of the airplane. He could tell the moment that the pilots gave full power to the Skytrain's two propellers. The C-47 began to shake and he could feel the vibrations even under the multiple layers of equipment and supplies now tethered to his body:

Four "D Rations" — 4 ounce vitamin B saturated chocolate bars. "Eat slowly," the instructions read. The meal should last "about half an hour."

Three "K Rations" — water-sealed boxes with one breakfast, dinner and supper unit inside. Canned meat. Four Chesterfield cigarettes. Matches. Crackers. Chewing gum. A dried biscuit. Halazone tablets to purify water. Wool socks. Two Mk II hand fragmentation grenades for ground contact with enemy personnel, two No. 82 Gammon grenade to take out their guns and fighting vehicles.

His M-1 rifle and two pouches of ammunition. A compass. A bayonet. More cigarettes. A pistol. A reserve parachute, stored in a pouch across his shoulders. His helmet, with camo netting on the outside, a map tucked inside, under the lining.

A canteen, a gas mask, sulfa pills for phosphorous burns. A bright yellow life preserver.

Twenty minutes before the drop. The crew chief went up and down the aircraft shaking and shouting each man awake. "We're almost over France!" He removed the C-47's door and a blast of cold air startled the rest of the drowsy crew alert.

Four minutes to the drop: The pilot lit the red flashing jump light. Terry's aircraft was at 1,500 feet — higher than the rest of the aircraft and separated from them. The whole first wave hit an unexpected cloud bank at the coast of France and quickly lost formation. The first aircraft ducked under it, giving their men only a 600-foot jump. Terry's aircraft climbed. With three minutes before the jump the men were standing clipped to their center line and the plane was heaving as tracer fire illuminated the clouds and reflected off the interior of the aircraft. The flak and shells leapt at the passing airplanes with a scream and popped into bursts of shrapnel and smoke.

At 1:18 a.m. the jump light flashed green. "Let's go! Let's go!" Terry and the others pushed out the door into the cold blast of air from the plane's engines. Everything he had secured to his body pulled and fell, spilling cartridges and mess kits and rifles into a rain of men, supplies and silk over the tracer-streaked fields below.

***

A thousand miles away, Dick was en route to Ploesti, piloting his B-24. They were only minutes from target when an explosion of sound and flak flashed with a temporary blinding burst.

The fuselage filled with shredded metal as the bomber heaved sideways. My grandfather whipped his neck around to co-pilot and crew.

"No. 2 engine hit!" "No. 3 losing power!"

The plane started to drag behind. Its tail turret was destroyed and they'd lost most of their aileron control.

"We have to ditch!" a crewmember yelled. "We can get back to base!" the engineer said.

My grandfather looked at the horizon and the smokestacks. He knew in their weakened state their B-24 wouldn't be able to keep speed with the rest of the protective pack and would likely be picked off by German fighters.

But he did not turn for base. He feathered No. 2 and increased power to the rest. He looked with intensity at his co-pilot, gripped the yoke and began his bombing run for Ploesti.

Attacked by twelve enemy aircraft in withdrawal, the engineer was severely wounded and rendered unconscious and Captain Harris, disregarding his own personal safety, revived him and rendered first aid, then returned to the controls and so skillfully maneuvered his plane that two of the enemy attackers were destroyed and the balance driven off. When a forced landing seemed imminent, Captain Harris refused to abandon his plane and wounded companion and skillfully utilized remaining power and fuel that a safe landing was affected at home base."

This was the narrative of his Distinguished Flying Cross. I got it years after I'd started the quest to find my grandfather. I was visiting Abuela's California house again when she handed me a manila folder.

"Here, darling, I found these papers for you, I thought they would be helpful."

Yes, they would have been really helpful, I thought silently. Inside was every form and detail I'd never had. It was the documentation and the units and the missions I'd hunted for years.

And the narrative of his Distinguished Flying Cross. When I first got it, the sheet was pure joy.

His Distinguished Flying Cross ... was earned on D-Day.

This was a hero story to brag about. This was exactly the type of armor I'd so badly wanted when I first flipped through his pages with a glass of wine, so many years ago.

But the journey to find my grandfather's past had taught me a tempering truth. There was no such thing as a perfect war story.

In my grandfather's memoirs, instead of a paragraph about the importance of his D-Day mission, I read this:

"Four days after Rome fell to allied troops I drove in," Dick started.

In Rome he met up with a military contact and checked into an officer's hotel on Via Veneto. Then Dick went out to secure women for both of them.

"It was so simple," Dick wrote. "Just wait in front of the hotel as beautiful girls strolled by, mostly in singles but sometimes in pairs. It was pick out the most beautiful, and then 'bouna sera, signorina.' The operative word was 'mangiare.' Most of them hadn't had a square meal for some time. (They all said they did not date German soldiers but I took that with a grain of salt. They frequently came from good families and they ranged from a few natural blondes through light browns to jet black, with pubic hair to match. There was never any payment except food, dinner in the evening and breakfast the following morning."

Rome fell June 4, 1944.

More, in the gray boxes of the Archives on June 6, 1944, my grandfather's name wasn't in there.

Why weren't you in the boxes? Why are you highlighting a woman's bed in Rome on June 8, if you were in the skies over Ploesti June 6?

I wrote about that flight, he said back. *I was there.*

I looked again. *There must be something I'd missed.*

The 98th's pilot's roster of that day recorded 35 names. Richard C. Harris wasn't one of them.

I went back into the Archives to re-examine the records for the 98th's mission reports of June 6, 1944.

The boxes held their story: Thirty-five planes went up. The 98th led the mission and as they approached their target, those 98th planes linked up with the 376th, 450th and 449th bomb groups to pound Ploesti.

Dick's childhood best friend Maj. Bill Sawyer was there. He was commanding the squadron and leading the attack that day.

I thought of Kolfage, and his loyalty to Cortez.

Did you get in a bomber that day and fly with the formation, unwilling to let your best friend go into war alone?

Did you just not bother with the paperwork? Do you not know me now, granddaughter?

A notation on one of the bomb group's mission reports caught my eye.

9:40 a.m., returning from target, Lt. James Plane reported, "Heard reported from command that strange B-24 was hanging back of formation, with no visible markings."

Was this you?

"I made several Ploesti raids," my grandfather wrote in the final pages about his war. "On one of them I got an engine shot out just before reaching the target. I flew over the target anyway and dropped my bomb load. En route back we were attacked by fighters and my engineer got creased in the head. After American fighters came to our rescue, I turned the controls over to my co-pilot and bandaged my engineer. The top turret was a bloody mess."

It was the same story as the Distinguished Flying Cross narrative.

"Attacked by twelve enemy aircraft in withdrawal, the engineer was severely wounded and rendered unconscious and Captain Harris, disregarding his own personal safety, revived him and rendered first aid, then returned to the controls ...."

Five years into my quest, I knew how incomplete the records were at the Archives. Some of the records sank when a ferry carrying the 98th's paperwork back to the U.S. was lost at sea.

Others burned in St. Louis. Some, for lack of a pencil or other bureaucratic mistake didn't record the right names, and the men who flew those missions were totally lost to history.

I went back to the stack.

Thirty-five planes went up that day.

The Archives only had the reports for 31 of them.

***

I lost Terry shortly after his jump. The official reports in the Archives sometimes contradicted themselves, and the books and memoirs on the topic were also mixed.

Terry's jumpmaster on Neptune 5 was 1st Lt. Roy Kessler. In the official report filed by Pathfinder commander Capt. Frank Lillyman a month after the operation he reported that Kessler, Terry and the others assigned to light Drop Zone C landed and had their Eurekas assembled by 12:37 a.m.

The mission report of Terry's plane says the men did not jump until 1:18 a.m.

I knew he and the men in Neptune 5 fell accurately on their assigned drop zone, where so many of their other Pathfinders did not. Neptune 5's men landed in orchard fields between the two French villages of Hiesville and St. Marie Du Mont, just a few hundred yards off target.

I knew Terry was one of the lucky ones who did not die by gunfire on the way down or crash into a tree or get picked off as he stood for the first time in those vulnerable seconds after his body hit the earth in a roll of straps and motion. I knew this because in letters the family received after his death, some of his former Easy Company paratroopers wrote of the joy they had when they saw him walking up a French road in the days after the drop.

But then he disappeared.

Maybe Terry landed in some of the ditches the Germans flooded with water. Maybe in a road or in a hedgerow. Drop Zone C was riddled with German rifle pits; I knew there was literal fire all around him. So many men who survived later wrote about the buildings the Germans set on fire to blind the planes and swallow falling paratroopers.

I knew he still had the Eureka. And the men with him had at least two of the holophane lights. A regimental study of the 506th's performance during those first hours of invasion, written a month after the battle, reported that the men successfully assembled those lights and radioed the planes.

But it also said those beacons did not help.

"At Drop Zone C ... the planes carrying the Second Battalion simply overshot the mark; the paratroopers knew when it happened. They saw three large green "T's" formed of electric lights pass under them and they recognized the zone markers that had been set up by the Regiment's Pathfinders. Still the beacon did not alarm the pilots ... when the men at last got their jump signal, the Battalion came to Earth with its center about 5 miles from Drop Zone C."

Terry was operating the Eureka, making sure it was pulsing. He and a protective rifleman were on their stomachs in the field to evade gunfire as 900 transport aircraft roared overhead flooding the sky with the parachutes of 14,000 men.

After the aircraft passed, he and the others began assembling randomly with other scattered units to head to assigned regimental checkpoints. No one was marching with the men they'd trained with. Those men were dead or likewise trying to regroup in the dark, as they encountered groups of Germans and flopped fast to determine the direction of the guns and return fire.

When they reassembled, they were told the next objective: They had to take the village of Carentan.

It's on that road to Carentan that Terry rejoined some of his brothers from Easy Company.

"The last time I saw T.C. he came trudging down a dusty lane — all smiles —and I was so glad to see him that I cried," former Easy Company brother and best friend Sgt. Burr Smith wrote to Annette. "Actually cried with relief to see him. I thought he was gone D-Day, and to see him was heaven on Earth."

The village of Carentan was surrounded by marsh, deep streams, uncovered fields and four bridges. The deadly battle that followed became known as the Carentan Causeway Fight. The Causeway was 40 feet across. It was an exposed, dusty highway that was only built up about six feet above watery marshes on either side.

"A rifleman may walk along this bank, perhaps stumbling and slipping into the water occasionally," the 502nd reported in its own regimental unit study after the Caretan fight. "There is not enough dirt on the right embankment to permit troops to dig in."

The four bridges on the way in were chokepoints. A place to die. Some soldiers swam under, thinking it was safer and found that "the canals [beneath them] all run with fair swiftness and are deep-to-drowning," the regiment reported.

What most threatened the approach, however, "was the complete exposure of the Causeway. Running straight as a die and standing boldly above the marsh, it was a high-perfect target to the enemy from three directions. Snipers might hide in the reeds on either side," the Regiment reported.

It was somewhere in this battle for Carentan that Terry was hit by sniper fire. The date wasn't clear. Smith's letter said Terry was killed in the same action that wounded Smith; which placed Terry's death on June 12, 1944.

Bullets hit Terry's head, near his jaw. They ripped into his right upper arm and his lower right leg, and he died.

Four years of government paperwork followed. Respectful yellow-sheeted letters home to his father, disbursement of final pay; decisions on a final resting place. But those 52 pages were short on closure. They listed three additional dates of death: June 13th, June 14th, and June 18th, 1944.

June 18, 1944, was the date of Terry's burial. His body was transported six miles north and east of Carentan, 21 miles southeast of Cherbourg. His body was placed in the newly dug and growing U.S. temporary burial grounds. U.S. Military Cemetery #1, Ste Mere Eglise, Plot D, Row 6, Grave 111.

The men who placed him in that grave couldn't identify him through his dog tags. Those were gone. They found his pay book, PFC. Terrence C. Harris, serial number 19091437.

They went through his effects, cataloged and stored them for return to his father.

A discolored ring on his hand. Two photographs. Terry's rosary.

A leather note case.

His father's silver pipe cleaner.

I found Terry once more, 70 years later. He was in the Archives, listed in the Quartermaster's rolls of the dead under "Report No. 97."

His was the 1,643 U.S. service member's death recorded that week.

18

Resolution

Col. Bill Sawyer and Dick, 1960s.

T he stacks would never conclusively tell me where or when Terry died. They would not provide proof on

Dick's Distinguished Flying Cross. But they would offer a gift, and then open the door to something else.

I was trying one last time on the Distinguished Flying Cross. I'd hired a researcher at Maxwell Air Force Base, and I was looking through every notation in my grandfather's official file. There had to be something.

I found it on Sept. 13, 1944.

That was the day that Dick earned an Oak Leaf Cluster for his Distinguished Flying Cross. In the paperwork it says he got it for successfully bringing his bomber to target under "very heavy, intense and accurate enemy anti-aircraft fire which severely damaged his plane."

In the mission paperwork Dick filled out when he landed, he'd reported "20 holes in plane."

You can't get an Oak Leaf Cluster for an award you haven't earned. So I was back in the Archives, hoping my grandfather might have left one last clue.

On Sept. 13, 1944, all four bomb groups of the 47th Wing – the 449th, the 450th, the 98th and the 376th were airborne on a mission against the Avisio Rail Road Viaduct in Italy. The 98th was leading. Flying lead was 98th Commanding Officer Col. Salvatore Manzo. My grandfather was his co-pilot.

I often found Manzo and my grandfather on the same bomber. Maybe they were friends, too; of the dozen photos that survived in his photo albums of the war, there was a photo of Manzo and my grandfather, sharing cigars.

Still, since Manzo was the commanding officer of the group, when I saw his name on the manifest, I sat up and took notice.

The mission pre-brief was a little different this time.

Bombing will be done by boxes. Let's make this 300th Mission one to be remembered for complete destruction of the target. The Group has a beautiful opportunity to score since we lead the Wing. Be certain we have proof with good pictures!

"Have you checked to see if there's a film?"

Film?

I was chatting with one of the Archives' historians about this mission, and he had another idea.

"On the fourth floor — films. They might have tape of the mission, since it was the 300th."

A few hours later I was in a dark film room at the Archives. There, amid reels of preserved 16 mm and 35 mm film was the unbelievable "300th Mission of the 98th."

After a few mishaps that sent spits of 16 mm film flying off the viewing tables, I got a hang of the projectors.

It was a silent film. So when I turned off the room lights, the only sound was the whir of the projector and the snap of film as it whisked around the wheel.

The film started with each bomber in line for takeoff, again making the slow, cumbersome taxi, almost like an elephant walk. Always lurching, then seesawing, always nose-to-tail.

The camera panned the taxiway, where the unending line of 98th Bomb Group Liberators and their crews waited to launch again.

No .... I scrambled to hit the reel's "stop" button before the frame sped away. Then I fumbled to rewind.

I double-checked the 300th's mission sheet. Looked at each name. Each serial number. Twice. I didn't want to fool myself and see something that was not there.

On the report that day, only one 98th bomber was coded "L" on the tail. It was right in front of me.

When I hit "play," I could barely see the screen through my tears. Capt. Richard Conant Harris was in 626-L, turning his bomber into the wind. He gunned his four Pratt and Whitneys, and that 16 mm film followed his bomber down the runway as it launched flat and fast into the Italian sun.

I am glad you finally see me, he said.

***

There was no way to capture that joy other than to work to ensure others would experience it too. In the process of searching for my grandfather's war story I'd photographed more than 30,000 Archives records. I'd built a website for them, too. On nights after I came back from another records haul, I'd write to my online friends that new photographs were about to go up. The best days were when I could find someone's father, when I could find their grandfather. I would relive the joy of finding my own. I'd post each one of those records up for free. I considered it my grandfather's gift: a history of the war for both bomb groups he served with, one mission report at a time.

Whether it was getting culled by data mining bots, by researchers, veterans' families or all three — that website got busy. 900,000 hits. 1 million hits. Emails started to come in, so many like this:

"My Dad never talked about the war ... now I know. Thank you."
The photos had connected me to Bill Sawyer, too. He would die in spring of 2010. But not before I'd emailed his children and sent them pages and pages of missions I'd photographed of his war service from the Archives. In the last months of his life, when his eyesight and health had failed, his children read them to him.

So by the time I was struggling to find more proof of my grandfather's Distinguished Flying Cross, many of the men in the squadrons he'd flown with were familiar to me. I knew their names. I would smile when I saw they were up in the air for another mission.

They became like ushers.

This way, this way, they'd whisper. *You are getting close ...*

When I saw them die, it left a hollow ache.

Many of those men were in the air with my grandfather and Bill Sawyer on June 6, 1944. *Lt. Donald D. Pucket. Lt. James R. Plane. Lt. Raymond J. Baker.*

Lt. Pucket was killed a month later, July 9, 1944, again over Ploesti.

"Pucket was hit by flak on bomb run between fuselage and No. 2 engine," Lt. Sidney Paisner wrote in the official record of that crash.

Paisner was in an aircraft on Pucket's wing. The bomber looked like it was holding; *they could make it,* Paisner thought. Then Pucket's plane started to fall out of the sky.

"The ship appeared to lose altitude rapidly. About 1,600 feet a minute," Paisner wrote.

Paisner drew his own bomber alongside; both aircraft were about 6,000 feet from the ground.

"We followed him down and drew abreast," he said. "There were about four or five men standing, apparently giving aid to an injured man on the floor. We waved to them, and an enlisted man lifted a bandaged hand and waved back. We drew alongside the cockpit ... the pilot's side was empty and Lt. Jenkins, the co-pilot, was flying right side by himself."

Paisner assumed Pucket, the pilot, was hurt. But Pucket wasn't hurt. He was in the back of his Liberator, trying to calm his crew and get them to jump.

The direct hit had ripped off the left side of combat photographer Staff Sgt. Leon Fourens' body; he died on the waist floor. The burst also flayed the skin off gunner Staff Sgt. Hershel Devore's face and blinded him with flak and plexiglas. Devore was dazed and nonsensical. Fourens was dead. Two others, the tail gunner and the flight engineer were unhurt, but they were too hysterical to move.

In the last seconds of the flight Pucket and the rest of the crew tried to tie parachutes onto the injured. Pucket paced up and down the catwalk, ordering them out. Devore wouldn't budge. The frightened and blinded nose gunner gripped the bomber instead and wouldn't let go.

Oh God, he's not going to make it, Paisner thought. He tried to get the co-pilot's attention once more, but Jenkins just waved him off.

The rest of the crew gave up and jumped past, tumbling out of their descending bomber. Only Jenkins, Pucket, the injured Devore and the two frightened crew remained.

Pucket pushed back into the cockpit and ordered his co-pilot to bail out. If he couldn't get his crew to jump, he would stay and fight the plane to the ground to give the wounded and the scared the best chance at survival.

The last words Jenkins heard from Pucket were instructions: "Take charge of the men and head for the hills," Pucket said. "I am going to stay with these hysterical dying men."

Through intelligence reports the 98th learned that Pucket's body was found in the wreckage by a Romanian Catholic priest. The crew could not retrieve the body in enemy territory. But the priest promised to conduct a funeral for Pucket at the crash site.

Pucket was posthumously awarded the Medal of Honor.

Lt. Plane was also killed over Ploesti, on August 18. Lt. Baker's plane was shot down in the same attack. My grandfather was in the air with them both on that mission, flying in "The Witch."

What did you think when these planes went down, yet life was so good to you?

***

In Iraq, and especially in violence-riddled Anbar province, IEDs and mortars played a same dangerous roulette with the men and women assigned there. I remembered another trip, to Kirkuk. To get to the rows of sleeping trailers, you had to walk by the trailer that had been the unfortunate recipient of an incoming rocket. It pierced right through the roof, killed the guy in bed.

"His number was just up," the guys on base said.

In Kirkuk when alarm went off for detected incoming, only the soldiers ran to the bunkers. And that's only because they were ordered to. The contractors just kept sauntering by. They were men who had meetings or breakfasts to get to; a detachment to risk had taken hold. It was a disorienting reality.

In late 1944, my grandfather succeeded his best friend Bill Sawyer as squadron commander. Lt. Herb Elliott became his intelligence officer. On a trip to headquarters the two were bribed by another officer who wanted to use the squadron's formation plane to smuggle cargo.

The officer "arranged a private apartment for us, dancing girls and all. I recall two girls doing a strip tease for us, then going to bed with us," Dick wrote.

The next morning, the officer told him that if they'd take their plane to Rome and unload some cargo, they'd be rich.

"I declined," my grandfather said. "I didn't report him only because this sort of thing was so prevalent."

The bribe reminded me of the greed I'd seen in Baghdad, and

I had a thought. I'd made an early mistake of idealizing war in Iraq. But I'd idealized my grandfather's war too.

Neither fight could ever be anything more or less than the men and women caught up in it. It was imperfect and flawed and full of opportunities for some, loss for others. It was hopefulness, sex, disappointment, sacrifice, unfairness, waste and mismanagement, valor and confusion. It was none of these things all of the time, because people are not these things all of the time.

In England war was breakfasts of beans that expanded into mission-ending farts at 20,000 feet. It was those Italian women, with their silky blonde, brown and black pubic hair even as it was my grandfather's courage to launch day after day against a target that would not die. It was a life-changing opportunity, a bigger paycheck and a ticket out of town. It was the selflessness of Lt. Donald Pucket and Terry's stand as an NCO. It was also corrupt officers or civilians who abused the system and it was bad command decisions that took lives. It was the missing paperwork that would always leave my grandfather's Distinguished Flying Cross with unanswered questions, and my great uncle's war with a death lost to history. It was a bureaucratic mess that was no better in 1944 than it was in 2010.

The Iraq War was the snarkiness of an Embassy Baghdad deputy chief of mission who complained that the tomatoes on Iraq's supply trucks weren't fresh, even as it was the utter selflessness of a lone soldier who threw himself on a grenade in a lifesaving act of valor. It was relationship-ending affairs like mine, at the same time it was the triumph of little girls' schoolhouses built with a hope for a country's future. It was the reality that won some veterans a seat in Congress and left others suffering alone on dirty couches, coughing up metal from too much time near Iraq's burn pits.

So many of the people who followed our soldiers into war —
and even some of the soldiers themselves — knew this too. They
decided that in this blindly unfair place, you should "get yours"
before your number was up. To not be the last soldier in Iraq.
To not be the one left holding the bag.

But just as many men and women signed up and went in when
Iraq was at its most dangerous. They, like Kolfage, volunteered
for the harder spots. A lot of them didn't come home.

And both groups were thanked for their service.

See, I told you it didn't matter ... my grandfather said.

My first experience with war was a naive one. Before I got on
the ground, war had been as distant to me as my grandfather's
memory. I'd expected more of myself and everyone else involved.
I'd scorned defense contractors as a prime reason for soaring
costs. Then Iraq's IEDs got more vicious, and with them, a
national demand to better equip each service member. Those
same contractors answered the call. No more exposed Humvees.
The forces would roll in heavy, in new V-shaped hulls known as
Mine Resistant Ambush Protected vehicles.

My grandfather nudged again.

Willow Run too had risen to Roosevelt's call. The B-24
Liberator would become the most-produced warbird in U.S.
history.

There were 18,000 Liberators assembled before the end of the
war.

Seventy years later the MRAP saved countless lives. There
were 18,000 of them in Iraq.

Our wars go on, forever connected to the past. In 2016 the 98th
Bomb Group reactivated one of its squadrons with B-1 bombers
from Dyess Air Force Base in Abilene. In 2010 the Air Force

did the same with the 343rd Liberator squadron my grandfather commanded after Bill Sawyer. Its legacy is carried on by B-52 strategic bombers from Barksdale Air Force Base in Louisiana.

New generations of pilots and ground crews are still flying in combat missions, now over Syria. And Afghanistan, Iraq, Yemen, Libya, and Somalia. New generations of young Texas airmen are still deploying overseas to guard the flight lines as their modern warbirds launch to strike. Fighter aircraft and swept wing bombers provide protective cover for shadows — U.S. special operations forces in combat against a terror without boundary.

Almost every bomb crews drop in this war has laser-guided precision. But there is still no such thing as a clean war. Civilians die. They did in 1944 and they did again in 2016. War is still costly and unpredictable. It still has missing swaths of history that may never see daylight.

I know, because I'm back to being a reporter again. The war against the Islamic State in Iraq and Syria is a war dependent on information and perception. So it is a war fought in secret. Actual numbers of U.S. troops on the ground are not provided. Embeds are no longer allowed. The Pentagon and White House say the men and women on the ground there are in harm's way; they are loath to say they are back in combat. The building will swear each soldier is safely away from the front lines, behind Iraqis who lead the way.

Except our soldiers don't fight that way, and war has a way of redefining any lines we draw.

And just like in the Archives, when the Pentagon adds a new name to that hallowed list, I feel a hollowed ache.

When I first went to Iraq information and disinformation were plentiful. It was my own knowledge that was scarce. Now I know what to ask but the information is impossible to find.

The irony isn't lost on me. I'm back to trying to understanding war from a distance.

I looked back at the pages of my grandfather's memoir that had frustrated me for so many years and I saw them in a different light. Maybe the chaos and incoherence in his story was not just because that was how his mind was, but also because that's how war was.

Maybe that is why he, like so many others, never talked about their experiences when they came home. So many of us had assumptions about the war stories we expected to hear, and had questions with no answers when those expectations and reality didn't match.

In the same haul of papers where Abuela had handed me Dick's Distinguished Flying Cross citation, she also gave me an envelope, addressed by hand. It was a letter from Bill Sawyer. He had written it to Abuela on the news of Dick's death.

As boys and young men, Dick and I opened our life-long dreams to each other — military commissions as officers and gentlemen, fighting in the defense of our country. The lure of travel to strange and exotic far-off lands, the glory of flying, the thrill of adventure around the world; the fun of a life lived to its fullest; the deep- seated joy of the enduring love of a beautiful woman, and the pride of parenthood — those were our goals, not power or wealth."

When Bill Sawyer died, he still had a sketch of his best friend Dick Harris on his bedroom wall. Despite a career of seeing the darkest of humanity, the two men decided to enjoy its sweet fruits. That was the last lesson my grandfather left me.

There would be no clean resolution in the paperwork; not in his memoirs, not in the Archives. But I finally understood, I never should have expected one. The paperwork and the medals and the recognition were not what my grandfather's heroism was built on.

My family's story was only one of thousands affected by this war truth.

I looked at the records again on July 9, 1944, the day Pucket died.

In his last pilot lineup of Pucket's Medal of Honor life, his name was misspelled.

19

Full Circle

D
ick and Abuela, Argentina, 1949.

Dick didn't write a line about how he felt about Terry's death. The memoir pages of his later years, even when he had his own children, never mentioned the loss of his brother again. Terry was the memory my grandfather would not touch. What Dick did write was that after he got the news, he asked for a more personal role in killing.

He got it; Bill Sawyer was still his commander, and the three boys had grown up in Glendale together. Bill Sawyer had loved Terry too. So he reassigned Dick as a tail gunner and put a .50-cal in his hands. Dick shot from the rear of the aircraft, angry. He alienated his fellow pilots by yelling at them to get closer to the German fighters, forgetting that when he was at the yoke he too steered his bomber as far away from the threats as possible.

But the shooting didn't help. So Dick returned to flying status and kept at Ploesti, going back into the smoke and fire until that terrible target fell. Then, when Bill Sawyer's time as squadron commander ended in late 1944, Dick assumed the role.

By spring 1945 Dick's tour was close to ending; he could stay on if he wanted. *He would get another fast-tracked promotion if he stayed ...*

Dick decided to go home.

"I thought I owed it to Dad to stay alive," he wrote.

When he finally came home to his father and to Glendale, Dick tried to resume a normal life. But the town felt like a Hollywood movie set that was staged for someone else's life. Dick knew we would not see his brother. But Terry was everywhere, and Glendale was too tidy to understand.

Instead he took a temporary assignment in Washington State to help the Air Force out-process air crews. He struggled to keep life fast enough to not think about life without Terry. Dick did not want to leave the Air Force, but if he wasn't fighting, he wasn't sure what he wanted to do in it.

Then the phone call came.

It was 7:30 a.m. Dick was at the Bachelor's Officers' Quarters in Walla Walla, Washington, dripping wet from a shower.

On the other end of the line, the Air Attaché branch of the

Pentagon.

"A voice in halting Spanish asked me to tell him, in Spanish, how to tune an aircraft radio," Dick said.

Dick and Terry had grown up speaking both Spanish and English in their California town. So Dick, as usual, decided to throw a little attitude.

"In fluent Spanish I answered that I couldn't even tell him how to do that in English, but if he wanted to know whether I could speak Spanish, then have at it," he wrote.

Dick was told to expect orders. He was going to spy school. The Air Force was about to open another door for my grandfather, to a new post-war life.

The U.S. had watched scores of German scientists and former SS officers flee Germany for Latin America, specifically to the welcoming government of Argentina's President Juan Perón. The U.S. wanted to keep tabs on all of these men, to lure as many of them into America's own defense programs as possible, and keep the rest from turning toward the rising Soviet Union.

After training, Dick arrived at U.S. Embassy-Argentina in July 1947 as a U.S. Air Force assistant air attaché. Publicly, he was to befriend the Argentine military, to observe and report any sightings of former SS officers.

Dick had another, secret assignment. To catch the trail of "the most dangerous man in the world," Otto Skorzeny.

Skorzeny was Hitler's top commando. He was the man who freed Mussolini. The embassy's reporting lit up with sworn leads:

Skorzeny was in Argentina.

Skorzeny was Eva Peron's secret bodyguard. Skorzeny was Eva's lover.

No rumor was too great for this war beast. Skorzeny was the

ghost who eluded them all. Dick was assigned to find him.
***

Truth, there were many women in my grandfather's life. But there was only one he called "Mi Vida." Of the chapters in his mind, this was his favorite. He re-edited his text, so that the night he first met Abuela was "Chapter One."

Dick peered over the edge of his box of memories and dove in happily. He was young again, clean-shaven and in dress whites. He was standing in the entryway to the dining room of the Consul General's house in Buenos Aires. It was Dec. 3, 1947.

These were the memories he wanted to live in.

It was the first U.S. Embassy-Argentina holiday party of the season, and Dick and two other intelligence officers drank ahead of time, bragging to each other about the night ahead. As they arrived, they stopped at the entryway of the Consul General's house to survey the female party goers inside, looking for their next prize.

"But I could only see one person," Dick wrote. "She was wearing a black off-the-shoulder dress which accentuated every curve. Her head was tilted back in gay repartee, her flashing hazel eyes were twinkling, and dark brown hair hung slightly to her shoulders."

Abuela had come to the U.S. Embassy-Argentina in 1944 as a clerk and typist. She and her mother Yolanda had moved from their native Chile to work there after Abuela had graduated from high school. She was already a favorite at the embassy, the one everyone called "sunshine."

That evening Abuela wore a black fitted Christian Dior "New Look" dress, with a long full skirt that bounced with the joy of fabrics that were no longer rationed by war. She had a deep tan and high black heels.

Dick's two fellow officers had seen her too. They turned to each other and made one more fateful $5 bet on who would be first to get her to dance.

My grandfather was last.

"It was the best bet I ever lost," he said.

The words in this part of my grandfather's memoir text were effusive, like a dream. He even wrote that as he took her hand, the small embassy band struck up "Heaven, I'm in Heaven."

"I'm going to marry you," he told her, with an intensity that told her he meant it.

Terry would have loved you, he thought.

Winning her became his next mission. He gave everything he had to the task. A few weeks after they met he threw his own Christmas party, inviting Abuela and Yolanda. The strategist in him knew he had to win her mother over too.

"I was dancing with Dick and he kissed me in front of everyone including my mother. I was, needless to say, astonished," Abuela said. "He then explained we had danced under the mistletoe. I had no idea of that American custom."

"It was our first kiss and it was a long one," Dick wrote. "Again I felt the refrain, "Heaven, I'm in Heaven" twirling from my brain down to the tips of my toes."

Dick used his housing allowance to rent a large villa, complete with a pool, and filled it with animals he collected to charm his new girl. An army of creatures wild and domestic grew. Dick captured a leopard cub orphaned by their hunt and brought it home to Abuela's delight, feeding the cub through a beer bottle with a baby nipple until it strengthened. He housebroke him by teaching the cat to use the shower floor.

"But my god, what a stench," Dick wrote. "The urine of wild cats stinks like the very devil." He took the cub to cocktail lounges and let it walk up and down the bar, startling customers. He took it to embassy cocktails, where he was the big hit. He added two baby ostriches to the mix and a menagerie of other furry creatures that Abuela adored. On days spent at their home she would roll around on the grass as her favorite, Marco Polo the hunting dog, and the rest of the zoo played along on long, leisurely afternoons together.

Dick brought her into his endless nights of spy work: entertaining the expatriate community and every Argentine and German officer he wanted to keep tabs on. He made her a part of his world.

"We'd be having martinis and drinks ... and all of those officers knew Daddy so well because he was a liaison with them, they would just come up to the house. If they saw the lights on at midnight they'd knock and come in with their drinking."

On those nights Dick plied them with liquor and quail from his latest hunts and generous strips of Argentine beef that rotated for hours on a backyard spit. Abuela would start a large paella cooking on the outdoor fireplace and giggle as half-dressed guests danced along Dick's villa pool, eventually falling in. The parties went round and round like this until early in the morning, and as the revelers drank, Dick would ask my grandmother to go around and take party photos of everyone in attendance.

"So I did, and had a ball, never realizing Dick was collecting this information," Abuela said. "Two times neighbors called the police. We'd dance and make music and I'd cook the paella on the porch on the back, and we'd all sit around and watch the paella as it cooked. One time one of the Argentines had had too much to drink. We had a big doghouse for our German Shepherd, and Dick said to the Argentine, 'Now, you behave yourself!' — they were the same rank and everything! He told him, 'Go sleep in the dog house!' And the Argentine did! He climbed into the dog house! We had a fit watching him, it was that kind of party. It was incredible. That's why the neighbors got mad, but they would ask me afterwards, 'What were you cooking last night? It smelled so good!'"

Dec. 3, 1948, a year to the day that they met, Dick and Abuela were married in the rear gardens of the U.S. Embassy-Argentina. December was summer in Argentina, and the young couple was already becoming a familiar sight in Buenos Aires' society pages. The newspapers all document the day: her dress, her flowers. The attendants. Four hundred people were invited, even the Peróns. They did not come, of course, but Juan and Eva Perón did send a case of French champagne, "which started to get to the guests rather quickly," Dick said, in a surviving 16 mm film the family kept for years of their wedding.

The next morning the phone in their honeymoon suite rang.

Dick returned to his new bride with a suggestion.

"Let's go see Marco Polo one more time before we depart on our honeymoon," he said.

They loaded their luggage into his car. Abuela's suitcase was small, compact. My grandfather's luggage … was not. It included guns, ammunition, fishing gear, cameras and camping equipment. He told her they were headed for little villages in the Andes, where there were lots of secluded spots to skinny dip.

"The scandal!" Abuela teased. "Don't you know I am a married woman?"

Inside, she wondered about her crazy new husband.

"It seemed odd to me, and I thought to myself, 'How different these Americans are!' But I didn't care, I was happy," Abuela said. When they pulled up to the house, fellow embassy attaché John Strong was there to greet them.

Abuela gave him a happy hug and Dick told his friend he would be right back, but first he had a very important mission. He tossed Abuela over his shoulder and over the threshold, threatening to run all the way to the backyard and dump her in the pool.

After Dick departed to check on his guest, Abuela was swarmed by Marco Polo and every other four-legged creature in the house.

I am home, she thought happily.

A few minutes later, my grandfather returned. "Are you ready, darling?"

When they get back in the car, Abuela asked if everything was all right.

"Yes, yes, John just had some information he needed to share." My grandmother was content with this, she never pressed for more. It would be this chemistry that would mark the next decades of their diplomatic lives.

"Well then, ¡Vamos!" she said.

Dick grinned. His pretty bride would not know the difference between their honeymoon trekking through the mountains and his new mission.

We think he's in Mendoza, John told him before they drove off. *Be careful.*

Dick gunned the engine and turned the car west. Target assignment: Otto Skorzeny.

****

I spent Thanksgiving 2010 still married. It was an emotionless Thanksgiving that made us both miserable. After the meal, we went for a walk. We'd both tried. I'd spent more than a year since my choices in Austin trying to make up for the hurt I'd caused, trying to be perfect. He'd tried too.

We talked about a call for GAO volunteers for a six-month assignment to Baghdad. To watch the final drawdown of forces in Iraq, to see this war complete.

"If you take that, we're not going to be married anymore," he said.

A year before I would have just nodded, muted my inner gut and stayed. I'd doubted I could be something good, so I should just be this.

But I'd finished my grandfather's war story. I was okay with what I'd found. I was a different person now.

With four words, our marriage was over. "I'm going for it."

That December I went back to California, to Abuela. It was the last Christmas I would get with her. On her glass bistro, a pre-lit tabletop Christmas tree glowed in greens and reds. Cinnamon-scented candles burned in little crystal holders, and a paella rested on her stove, its mussels steamed, its yellow rice flat and full.

Abuela was in her late 80s, but she still dressed for dinner. She wore a silver choker, deep red lipstick that framed her expressive hazel eyes, and a splash of Chanel No. 5.

I'd spent years seeking my grandfather's story. I now spent more time asking about hers. On this visit we sat side by side at her retirement community pool, where steam rose from the heated waters as rows of elderly residents went through the motions of aqua aerobics. She took my hand to tell me about the diary pages of her own, about her childhood in Chile and the story of her mother Yolanda. I learned about how her life got harder, after the sheen of Dick's diplomatic life had gone.

It would be a disservice to her life to say their dating and marriage were perfect. The night they met, Abuela was in love with another man. Dick, even though he'd fallen in love, kept his options open. But there was something in them both that loved this partnership and forged it over 40 years and three daughters.

Among their tougher times there were many years of magic.

But there was also not a day that passed in their diplomatic life that did not deliver the social need to drink, and on the few events where no alcohol was allowed, my grandfather would find ways to sneak in bottles. At receptions he would always graciously accept one more, laughing while telling the room, "I regret that I have but one stomach to give for my country."

Just a hazard of the job, he said.

In 1964 he was passed over for promotion to brigadier general, and the show came to an end. In his memoirs Dick said the decision was the result of an internal investigation on a vacation rental which resulted in a $136 fine. There were no other details. It was the end of his official service to his country, and in it Dick concluded an ugly truth. There was nothing more to accomplish.

The salty youth who lived life out loud, who survived 63 combat missions but lost his brother and who spent more than 15 years as a Cold War spy had to live the rest of his life as a regular man.

And this, he said, in all earnestness, "triggered what evidently had been latent alcoholism. I began drinking quite heavily."

In those final visits with Abuela I learned how she survived his final years, when my grandfather spent days drinking in his white leather chair. He started thinking about his war. Pride and bravado surfaced fast and easy, as did his memories of all his women. Then glimpses of grief and loss. Each emotion and thought competed to be first and found voice in short bursts of stories of bombers and burning Scotch, camels and Jimmy Stewart. They found voice in little anecdotes about his brother, but not in the harder things.

If my grandfather had more time to live, if his mind and body had not failed him, would he have gone back to those pages to revise? Would he have cared to include the exact dates and bomb groups and the names of the men he flew with, or thought more about the story he wanted to leave of his war? I doubt it. I saw his final days as they were, with my grandfather bathed in window light that picked up dust specks and the swirl of his endless cigarettes. He sat lost in the memories of an extraordinary life that entered his watering eyes and heart in waves of emotion he tried to control and convey, sentence after sentence. I saw a glass tumbler speckled with ice and liquid that he sipped in

between thoughts, and I saw my grandmother at his side, her fingers perched, ready to type.

***

I left for Iraq again that July 2011. It was my longest stint there, and the strangest. I wasn't in a desert tent. I wasn't rolling along empty roads. I was at the U.S. Embassy complex with about 9,000 others. I wasn't a journalist or an outsider. I was part of the footprint now.

My partner for this assignment was Lisa McMillen, a fellow female GAO analyst, only 28. The exact age I was when I first came to Iraq in 2003. We were there to observe as soldiers raced to hand back so many bases and buildings that didn't exist eight years before. To let Iraq take its future into its own hands.

Our days could be anything: a helicopter ride north to observe columns of heavily armored vehicles start to convoy out; a scramble for a cement bunker if we got caught outside when the "duck and cover" alarm went off. Or it could be staring at the ceiling, a bit haunted in our beds as the "incoming" alarm rang out in the dark. We'd stay in our rooms, maybe laugh about meeting in the kitchen for glass of wine. Then we'd wait for the confirmation of the distant impact of indirect fire. Baghdad was a cafeteria that spilled with steaks and lobster on Sundays and endless embassy formals that women had gowns shipped into Baghdad for — through Amazon.

I admired that there was something in Lisa's soul that knew to soak up these months, to open her heart and mind wide to the soldiers and civilians who were along for this ride with her. This was something she would never see again. She had a slight limp, and her left arm was not as strong as it could be, due to muscle loss from a stroke that she'd beat back through years of determined physical therapy. She fought like hell to get this assignment and demanded to carry her own bags. She swung in and out of MRAPs and helicopters with a speed that dared anyone to try and ask if she needed help. We argued about what to do if we were ever caught outside during incoming, and she told me she would not accept the help — for me to get under cover as quickly as possible.

She is just like my first crew, I thought, others before self.

I knew it was hard for Lisa to understand why I often preferred to be a hermit on nights that she could not wait to get out. Why instead I watched from afar, why I left the party early.

The allure of war took an early, fast grip on me in 2003. It was through wiser eyes that I watched that same spell be cast on this latest group, eight years later at U.S. Embassy-Baghdad. The embassy was a fortress America, a pressurized pit of high policy stakes with thousands of men and women, so far from home. The excitement of war enveloped them too. The trysts that launched that fall, as they had every year before, became the tight-lipped fodder of friendships to last forever, because the people who went through this assumed no one back home would understand.

I finally understood it, and I didn't want to begrudge them the experience. But I still didn't want to go to dinner on those nights of steak and lobster, under festive bunting and enormous American flags. I wanted to honor war and the men and women who fought it for what it was, not how we wanted it to look. I knew that 2011 was no different than 2003 was no different than 1944. There was still cheating and drama, deaths and injury, greed and heroism. And always another drink at Baghdaddy's, the embassy bar.

Instead, I was just grateful. Often when Lisa was out, I was online, emailing. I was finally one of the lucky few attached to their cellphones, sending one last message and counting the days toward home.

We were halfway through our tour when we hit another milestone.

September 11, 2011. Ten years since four hijacked planes changed everything. Eight years since a dusty convoy into Iraq with four airmen from Texas. Seven years to the day since the rocket attack at Balad.

That afternoon a group of Marines honored a request. They raised a new American flag for me over U.S. Embassy-Baghdad, flown in honor of Senior Airman Brian Kolfage.

20

Wings

Manassas, Va., 2015

In May 2015 Bill stood in the sun, scanning for me amid a crowd five rows deep of WWII veterans, their families and hundreds of onlookers at Virginia's Manassas Regional Airport. That cute airport was a regular spot for us, where Bill took me flying in Cessnas all over the Chesapeake Bay when we finally got the chance to date.

The time since Iraq had sped by. I returned from Baghdad in December 2011; Bill and I married soon after. We traveled to that famous California beach at Hotel Del Coronado. As the Pacific surf pushed and pulled, and seagulls eyed our simple wedding feast, we dug our feet into the sand and clinked a toast as man and wife. A few floors above us, Sorenson sketched Willow Run from his oceanview hotel room. My grandfather darted about the clouds in a Liberator, and my grandmother watched over it all with love.

I went back to journalism, too, to tell the soldier's story from our bases in the U.S. and from spots all over the globe where our men and women continue to serve in the defense of our nation.

That was what brought us to Manassas that bright May day. I'd been working on a story for weeks on the Commemorative Air Force — pilots and volunteers all over the U.S. who spent their weekends and vacation time restoring WWII aircraft and flying them to air shows. The group had flown to airports in almost every state to get those bombers, fighters and transport aircraft near the remaining few veterans who were still alive. The veterans would come, often driven by children or grandchildren as a surprise gift, to fly a last honor flight. They'd bring their sheepskin -lined flight jackets. Boxes of letters.

Sometimes the more frail veterans would need help, and the volunteers would give them a hand up into the aircraft. But more often than not, something straightened last minute in those elderly warriors. Once they saw their bombers again they'd find the strength to climb in one more time, by themselves.

It was May 7, 2015. The airport's ramp was filled with dozens of World War II aircraft. They were lining up to take off for a practice flight. The next day they would fly over the National Mall in a sky parade of more than 100 aircraft to celebrate the 70th anniversary of Victory-Europe.

Down the ramp you could see almost every aircraft that

had a role in air combat. The long, silvery figure of the B-29 Superfortress, the airframe that ended the war. The unmistakable profile of the B-17 Flying Fortresses and B-25 Mitchells, bombers whose crews died by the thousands to make the Superfortress' final airstrike possible. Farther down the line, the ramp glittered with the "Little Friends," the fighter aircraft that had protected my grandfather's bomber from overhead. The yellow piercing noses of the P-40 Warhawk. The ferocity of the P-47 Thunderbolt. The unmistakable purr of the P-51 Mustang. I was riding in the Liberator; a B-24 named "Diamond Lil." She was one of only two remaining flying Liberators in the world, an aircraft loved and cared for by a Texas-based volunteer crew and proudly flown by Al Benzing, a retired Northwest Airlines and Delta pilot.

I picked a seat in back and buckled in. Later in the flight I would climb into the cockpit and say hi, the crew already knew me well. This moment was for a quieter time, for reflection.

I sat by the two large open windows where Lil's .50-caliber guns used to fire. The crew started up her four propeller-driven engines and Lil's belly filled with noise. I put my hands on the bomber's aluminum skin. I felt it buzz. Electric. The whole aircraft began to vibrate. Lil's tails jolted up and down as she lurched forward, just as she had 70 years before. I turned my face to the turret window and felt the hot air she blasted up into the fuselage from the sunny asphalt of our Northern Virginia airport.

We turned to the runway, and I gripped my grandfather's metal World War II pilot wings in my hands.

"Thank you," I said. Then Lil gathered speed and lunged for the sky.

Just before D-Day, June 1944

Terry and Pathfinders

Patricia Everson, inside Seething Control Tower.

—News-Press Photo

Cadet Capt. Richard C. Harris
He's Ready To Take Off Again

Flying Cadet Thrown Out Of Plane, Lands By Parachute

By FRANK KUEST

● True to army tradition, Cadet Capt. Richard "Dick" Harris, 21, was up in the air again today, recuperating from "the thrill of a lifetime" that he experienced yesterday. While receiving intricate acrobatic instruction from Lt. R. L. Scott of the United States army air corps, over the San Fernando valley yesterday, Harris was thrown from the rear cockpit as the plane whirled into an upside down position when Scott sent it into a "snap roll."

Finding himself on his own, 4100 feet above ground, Harris calmly surveyed the situation and, after waiting for innumerable seconds, yanked the rip cord of his parachute.

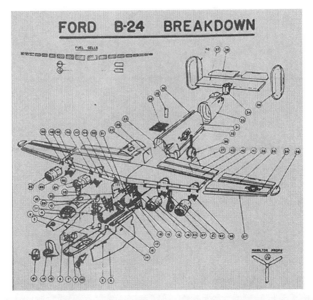

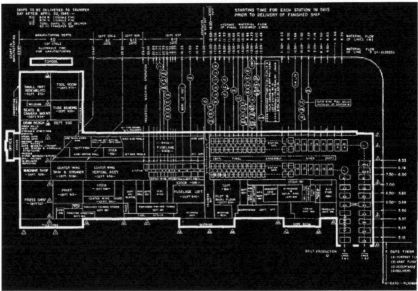

Sorenson's assembly line plan for Willow Run.

The Goodfellow AFB airmen of Linebacker 10, and the author.

21

Acknowledgements

I n Georgetown, Tennessee, there is a man named Herb
  Harper. In his own words, "he is well for an 85-year-old."
  He spends his mornings doing the usual chores, then goes
outside to mow his lawn on a 52" zero radius mower.

"I have slowed down considerably, as it seems the hills get steeper and the lanes longer," he told me.

After Herb's finished, he drives to the nearby nursing facility to help care for the love of his life, Joan. He wants to make sure she is still eating properly.

And then he comes home to his computer, where he is a lifeline for people like me.

For years any living WWII veteran of the 98th Bomb Group — and then their surviving children and grandchildren — have known to find Herb Harper.

Herb's journey with the 98th started in 1949. My grandfather had left the bomb group just a few years before. In 1949, he was in Argentina with Abuela. They had just welcomed their first child, my mother Monica Linda.

The 98th on the other hand, was getting ready to go back to war. This time in Korea.

The 98th wasn't flying Liberators anymore, even though it had only been four years since WWII ended. The 98th was a B-29 Superfortress bomb group now. Herb Harper served as one of its armament technicians. After he and the rest of the ground crews saw their modern, shiny bombers off, sometimes the men would just go sleep in the grass and wait for those warbirds to get back.

During the Korean War, Herb was detached from family. The young man did not grow up in a home that gave him voice. But he would tell me in emails how, in his 22 years in the Air Force, he found it. He also found his Joan and started a family of his own: Suzanne, Ian and Keith. Then he started to volunteer for the 98th Bomb Group Association, to make sure the voices of the rest of the men who'd served the group were never lost. He's been its heart and key historian ever since.

In 2009 he added me to the mix of people he helped, and together we built a library to the 98th. Without Herb, this book would not exist and I am not sure I would have found a path toward home.

He is one of many people in the following paragraphs I want to thank. First, the men and women who answer the call to serve our nation, not only those who flew the warbirds of the past but those who still serve today. Specifically, Senior Airman Brian Kolfage and the men and women of the 17th Security Forces Squadron at Goodfellow AFB, the 422 Civil Affairs Battalion, the 352nd Civil Affairs Command and the 101st Airborne Division. It seems that no matter what the conflict, the Screaming Eagles are there. Or, as my grandfather whispered when this journey first began: *All war is connected.*

Second, the many men and women who have dedicated their lives to making sure the war stories of the past aren't lost as we lose the soldiers who lived them, especially Patricia Everson, Jim Turner and Tom Brittan, who unfortunately passed away before this book saw print. The volunteers behind ArmyAirForces.com and B24bestweb.com, and everyday volunteers who have made knowing the Liberator's history their passion, including: Daniel Stockton, Bob Livingstone, Evan Thomas, Dan Studener, Ed Clendenin, Pete Johnston and Gino Künzle and many others. At Maxwell Air Force Base, Air Force Historical Research Agency's archivist, Archangelo "Archie" DiFante and researcher George Cully who were bottomless in their patience with my many questions. Pathfinder key historian David R. Berry. The military historians behind the reference desks of the second floor of the National Archives at College Park, Md. You are invaluable. And patient. Your knowledge of the treasures to be found within the thousands of gray boxes preserved there is humbling.

The authors who elegantly captured the stories of both bomb groups: USAF Col. Jeff Brett, the late Robert Dorr, U.S. Army Air Forces Maj. Bob Sternfels, pilot of "The Sandman" in the Aug. 1, 1943 Ploesti raid; and the talented authors who captured the stories of the paratroopers and Pathfinders of the 101st Airborne, "First to Jump" author Jerome Preisler and "We Who Are Alive and Remain" author Marcus Brotherton. The next generation: Vickie Croston, daughter of Rose "Rosie the Riveter" Leigh Abbott, known later as Rose Will Monroe. Susan Finn, the daughter of 101st Airborne, 506th Parachute Infantry Regiment Easy Company Sgt. Burr Smith. The family of Dick's best friend, Col. Willis Bruner "Bill" Sawyer. The family of Dick and Terry's sister, the late Annette Harris Turner.

The volunteer men and women of the Commemorative Air Force B-29/B-24 Squadron, who keep the B-29 Superfortress "Fifi" and her sister "Diamond 'Lil" flying, especially Allen Benzing, Paul Stojkov, Phil and Kim Pardon, Curtis Wester, Shad Morris and Jim Neill, and many others at CAF who spend their weekends making sure this generation doesn't forget.

The skilled authors I leaned on for help, especially two very special Dallas gals: college roommate and confidant Sarah Hepola, author of the *New York Times'* bestselling "Blackout," and Catherine Cuellar, lifelong cherished friend and published author in "Dallas Noir."

Editor and adviser Zach Schisgal. *Stars and Stripes* managing editor for content Tina Croley. Your keen eye made my copy better. The Scripps Howard News Service editors who sent me to Baghdad so long ago and my former colleagues at the GAO who still fight the good fight. Last, my colleagues now in the Pentagon Press Corps - you regularly inspire me.

Caroline Teagle for designing two stunning book covers, one

for the first edition and one for the second. I hope all my books are brought to life with your genius creativity.

My grandfather, the late Col. Richard C. Harris, who taught me about war, and my Abuela, Mónica Lahtz Harris, who taught me about love. Their remarkable daughters and spouses, my mother Monica Linda Hughes and her husband Joe Kelly Hughes, my aunt Denise Harris Troy and uncle Carl Troy, and aunt Cynthia Harris. My large Dallas family, especially my dad, Tony Copp. I inherited the perseverance to see this through from you. My sister Jackie Copp Gahagan, her husband Cole, and their children Annabel and Henry. Annabel, you have Abuela's deep dimples and her Chilean fire. Henry, there's a reason you love to be airborne. Your great-grandfather and great-uncle have you under their wings. My stepmother Kay Copp, brothers Troy Manson, Corey Manson and Alex Copp, sister-in-law Megen Manson, nieces Quinn and Addie, nephew Wyatt and sister-in-law Vicky Smithee. My 2011 Baghdad partner Lisa McMillen. It turned out your stroke masked an even bigger fight. I still miss you, but I will forever be awed by the grace and strength at which you faced your final challenge, this time against ALS.

Last and most importantly, to my husband Bill Hutchison. Thank you for picking me up from the airport in Austin in 2009, and for being part of the ride ever since. I love you.

22

Endnotes

C hapter 2: The Embed
1) Six days after "Shock and Awe"- Operation Iraqi
Freedom began on March 20, 2003 at 5:34 am local.
"Allied Participation in Operation Iraqi Freedom," by Stephen
Carney, Center for Military History, United States Army, 2011.

2) All Iraq scenes are from journal entries I recorded,
photographs I took, from follow-up outreach to the crew of
Linebacker 10 and from my coverage of the 17th Security Forces
Squadron, including the following articles, excerpts of which are
reproduced with permission from the E.W. Scripps Company:

3) "Locally Trained Pilots Fly Iraq's Skies," March 18, 2003;
"Goodfellow Crew First Air Force Squad in Iraq," March 28,
2003.

4) The outreach to media organizations: Bryan Whitman,
Deputy Assistant Secretary of Defense for Media Operations,
"Media Military Training Program," November 1, 2002.

5) Numbers of embedded reporters: U.S. Department of
Defense, "Embedding Statistics," from the Office of the Secretary
of Defense Freedom of Information Act Reading Room.

6) Total casualties taken from the U.S. Department of Defense,

both hostile and non-hostile deaths, Operation Iraqi Freedom and Operation Inherent Resolve, as of August 19, 2016.

Chapter 3: So This is War

7) All Iraq scenes are from journal entries I recorded, photographs I took, and double-checked with the crew of Linebacker 10, 422nd Civil Affairs Battalion Maj. Linda Scharf and Baghdad airfield commander Col. A. Ray Myers. Scenes are also taken from articles I wrote for my newspapers, which are reproduced with permission from the E.W. Scripps Company, including:

8) "Blackhawk Helicopter Crews Say Goodbye to Fallen Friends," April 12, 2003;

9) "Snipers Interfere With Red Cross Work," April 16, 2003.

Chapter 5: The Wound-up Punch

10) The description of Dick and Terry's childhoods is taken from the collected memoirs and photo albums of the late Col. Richard C. Harris.

11) Promotional pamphlet, "Glendale: Fastest Growing City in America" Glendale Chamber of Commerce, 1924. Stored at Calisphere, the digital collection of the University of California. http://content.cdlib.org/ark:/13030/c8pr7vbs/?layout=metadata

12) Glendale Branch, Security Trust & Savings Bank publicity department, First of the Ranchos: The Story of Glendale, 1924. http://content.cdlib.org/ark:/13030/c8222t49/?lay- out=metadata

13) John Underwood, Images of Aviation: Grand Central Air Terminal, Arcadia Publishing.

14) Adjutant General of the Army, Flying Air Cadets, Army Air Corps program manual, April 1940.

Chapter 6: The Five Dollar Bet

15) Sorenson's night in San Diego: Charles Sorenson, My Forty Years With Ford, Wayne State University Press, 2006.

16) Popular Science, Vol. 142, No. 5, "Look Out Hitler, Here Comes The Flood! Liberator Bombers Rolling Off Assembly Lines Show How Mass Production Will Swamp the Axis," Pgs. 78-85. May 1943.

17) How the bomber got its name: Popular Science, Vol. 142, No. 5, "She Isn't Much To Look At - But They Call Her The Liberator," Pgs. 86-91. May 1943.

18) Initial details on Sorenson's design for Willow Run and the bomber assembly: Warren Benjamin Kidder, Willow Run, Colossus of American Industry, KLF Publishing, 1995.

19) Initial details on Sorenson's design for Willow Run and the bomber assembly: Willow Run Reference Book, written by plant staff, Ford Airplane School Printing Department, Feb. 1, 1945.

20) The requirements to become an Air Cadet: Adjutant General of the Army, Flying Air Cadets, Army Air Corps program manual, April 1940.

21) Terry's dismissal is recorded in the collected memoirs and photo albums of the late Col. Richard C. Harris.

22) The story behind the five-dollar bet is taken from the Memoirs of Col. Richard C. Harris.

23) The description of Dick's wash ride is rebuilt from a magazine feature on the flight test: "Wash Ride," by Lt. Richard Ryan, Flying Magazine, 1943, pg. 88.

24) The newsclip on the fall: Frank Kuest, "Cadet Thrown Out of Plane, Lands By Parachute," The Glendale News-Press, 1940 article reproduced with permission, courtesy of The Los Angeles Times.

25) Air Corps News Letter, Vol. XXIII, July 1, 1940, No.

13, "Flying Cadet R.C. Harris, of Class 40-H … became the detachment's first emergency parachute jumper."

Chapter 7: Purple Hearts

26) All Iraq and San Angelo, Texas, scenes are from my own memory and double checked with Senior Airman Brian Kolfage, Airman First Class Valentine Cortez, 422nd Civil Affairs Battalion Maj. Linda Scharf; then-Maj. Michael Maguire, 352nd Civil Affairs Command. They were also contained in journal entries I recorded, photographs I took, and from my reporting, excerpts of which are reproduced with permission from the E.W. Scripps Company, including:

27) "Bechtel Gets Black Marks for Iraqi School Repairs," Dec. 8, 2003;

28) "Iraq Behind the Cameras: A Different Reality," Dec. 12, 2003; "United for the Journey: Pair to Marry After Groom Loses Legs, Hand, in Iraq," Oct. 17, 2004.

Chapter 8: The Search

29) Dick's journey through Canada and Sioux City and Terry's time with the Merchant Marines, from The Memoirs of Col. Richard C. Harris.

30) The re-creation of Terry's enlistment and assignment to the 506th Parachute Infantry Regiment is based information from the following sources:

a. Individual Deceased Personnel File, "Terrence C. Harris," provided courtesy of the U.S. Army Human Resources Command.

b. Steven Ambrose, "Band of Brothers, E Company, 506th Regiment, 101st Airborne From Normandy to Hitler's Eagle's Nest," Simon and Schuster.

c. Marcus Brotherton, "A Company of Heroes, Personal Memories about the Real Band of Brothers and the Legacy They Left Us," Penguin Group.

d. Marcus Brotherton, "Who We Are Alive and Remain: Untold Stories From the Band of Brothers," Penguin Group.

e. George Goodridge, 506th Parachute Infantry Regiment, Fox Company, "The Airborne Invasion of Normandy," a chapter from "Toccoa to Normandy to Berchtesgaden, A Proposed History of Fighting Fox Company," as preserved at the National Archives.

f. Jerome Preisler, "First to Jump, How the Band of Brothers was Aided by the Brave Paratroopers of Pathfinder Company," Penguin Group.

Chapter 9: Rose Leigh

31) First heavy bomber response: The Official World War II Guide to the Army Air Forces, Simon and Schuster, 1944, p. 329, "War Calendar," Dec. 9, 1941.

32) Only 33 left the assembly line: Army Air Forces Statistical Digest, World War II, Office of Statistical Control. p. 120: Heavy Bombers -Total, B-24. Dec. 1941.

33) The life story and photographs of Rose Leigh Abbott were provided courtesy of her daughter, Vickie Croston.

34) Additional historical background on Rose Leigh Abbott provided by independent researcher Anne H. Lee and used with permission.

35) The employment history of Rose Leigh Abbott provided by her daughter, Vickie Croston.

36) The floor plans and blueprints of Willow Run's assembly line and B-24 assembly provided by the Bensen Ford Research Center and re-used with permission courtesy from The Henry Ford.

37) Further description of the Willow Run facility drawn from Willow Run Reference Book, by Plant Guide Staff, Ford Airplane School Printing Dept., Feb. 1, 1945

38) 42,000 employees: "Work and Wage Experience of Willow Run Workers," Bureau of Labor Statistics Monthly Labor Review, Vol. 61, No. 6, December 1945. P. 1074.

39) 1.2 million parts: There is some discrepancy on how many parts there were in a B-24. The commonly cited number is 1.2 million. A Popular Science May 1943 in-depth feature on the Liberator said it was comprised of 1.25 million parts (Vol. 142 No. 5, pg. 80.); the Collings Foundation, which is one of two organizations caring for living Liberators, said there are 1.2 million. Ford's Willow Run Reference Book (p. 37) cites that there were 465,472 parts in a B-24J, including the plane's 313,000 rivets, but that count may have reduced all the individual pieces into the parts they comprised.

40) Complete description of the sizes of a Liberator's wingspan, tails and wheels found in Willow Run Reference Book.

41) Ammunition load for each turret found on page 60 of the Willow Run Reference Book.

Chapter 11: Let's Go to War

42) The search for my grandfather, discussion on "Greenpants" and discovery of A/C 42-52097 and crew: Screen shot of ongoing dialogue on ArmyAirForces.com WWII aviation experts forum, discussion January 5-6, 2010.

43) Signature sheet for "Lonesome Polecat," $305,711 price and Ford's Willow Run and the photograph of Dick's first crew, courtesy of U.S. Air Force Historical Research Agency, Maxwell Air Force Base, Alabama. Archangelo "Archie" DiFante, Archivist.

44) Description of what clothing the men packed for the journey: The Memoirs of Col. Richard C. Harris.

45) Take off procedure for B-24: Consolidated B-24 Bomber Pilot's Flight Operating Instructions, September 15, 1942; Periscope Film LLC 2006 and verified with current Commemorative Air Force B-24 pilot Allen Benzing.

46) Marrakesh crash: The Memoirs of Col. Richard C. Harris, chapter 3, p. 27., and U.S. War Department Missing Air Crew Report (MACR) for A/C 42-52108, Pilot Lt. Joseph Shank, including U.S. War Department correspondence to widow of crew bombardier Lt. Turner A. Sowell.

47) "Laki-Nuki" crash: The 448th Bomb Group (H), Liberators Over Germany in World War II, by U.S. Air Force Col. Jeff E. Brett, Schiffer Military History and found in The Memoirs of Col. Richard C. Harris.

Chapter 12: Greenpants

48) The story of what it was like to have the 448th Bomb Group in Seething is rebuilt from interviews with Patricia Everson for my 2013 story for Stars and Stripes, "One Woman's Devotion Keeps Memory of WWII Unit Alive," Sept. 9, 2013, which is reproduced in this chapter with permission. Additional details on Norwich and Seething provided through follow up interviews with Patricia Everson and Jim Turner.

49) Story of Dick and Terry's reunion in Seething: The Memoirs of Col. Richard C. Harris.

Chapter 13: Second Chances

50) The story of Kolfage's recovery and post-injury life is built from extensive interviews with Senior Airman Brian Kolfage, my own personal recollections and my reporting for E.W. Scripps

Company, reproduced with permission: "All About Attitude: After Brutal Injury, Airman's Moving On," March 15, 2005.

Chapter 14: An Uneven Spring

51) Bomber every 55 minutes: Associated Press article as run in the Sarasota Herald Tribune, "Plant Turns Out One Bomber Plane Every 55 Minutes," May 21, 1945, p. 3.

52) Visit of Walter Pidgeon: "Willow Run Guest Book," Jan. 21, 1944 sign-in. Stored at the Benson Ford Research Center, Acc. 435, Charles La Croix Records.

53) Hedley's Bar: Flight: Weekly Illustrated Magazine of Morrison Air Field Base, Vol. 1, No. 16, Nov. 1, 1941. Page 6. https://cmgpbphistoricalpalmbeach.files.wordpress.com/2010/09/morrison_field_nov_01_1941.pdf

54) That A/C 42-95075, "Happy Hangover" was built at Willow Run: "Steven Birdsall, Log of the Liberators, Appendix, Ford, Willow Run, pg. 313

55) Rose Leigh in the movie: Interview with Vickie Croston, Rose's surviving daughter.

56) Dick's recollections of flying over Europe in a Liberator: The Memoirs of Col. Richard C. Harris.

57) Missing Air Crew Report and death certificates for 2nd Lt. John Masters and the crew of 42-95075, "Happy Hangover," as recovered from Fold3.com historical records.

Chapter 15: The Day We Bombed Switzerland

58) The official U.S. State Department telegrams and documents surrounding the Schaffhausen bombing can be found here: https://history.state.gov/historicaldocuments/frus1944v04/ch6subch2

59) The chapter is rebuilt from The Memoirs of Col. Richard C.

Harris and from more than 300 pages of documentation, including mission reports, Missing Air Crew Reports, Interrogation Reports, Maps and Reports of Operations, and Dog Tags of the lost crews from that event.

60) All document pages specifically cited may be found here: http://www.taracopp.com/8th-Air-Force-448th-Bomb-Group/04011044

61) Specific mission reports, Interrogation Reports, and Missing Air Crew Reports used extensively in the narrative include: Operation's Officers Report, April 1, 1944: http://www.tara-copp.com/8th-Air-Force-448th-Bomb-Group/04011044/i-4WB-MJTm/A

62) 448th Bombardment Group: Formation Sheet Over Target http://www.taracopp.com/8th-Air-Force-448th-Bomb-Group/04011044/i-jjQvPdq/A

63) 448th Lead Navigator's Report, April 1, 1944: http://www.tara-copp.com/8th-Air-Force-448th-Bomb-Group/04011044/i- mTR4KCW/A

64) Lt. Harris Interrogation Report, April 1, 1944: http://www.tara- copp.com/8th-Air-Force-448th-Bomb-Group/04011044/i- GH8XczP/A

a. Lt. Cherry C. Pitts Interrogation Form, April 1, 1944: http://www.taracopp.com/8th-Air-Force-448th-Bomb-Group/04011044/i-5FVXvrh/A

b. Casualty investigation for Lt. Mellor's A/C 42-110087, including the death of Tech Sgt. William Warren: http://www.tara-copp.com/8th-Air-Force-448th-Bomb-Group/04011044/i-NmBQP3M/X3 and

65) Individual casualty questionaire: http://www.tara-copp.com/8th-Air-Force-448th-Bomb-Group/04011044/i-s4pcHLF/and

a. Casualty questionnaire with Tech Sgt. Francis Marx, http://www.taracopp.com/8th-Air-Force-448th-Bomb-Group/04011044/

b. The death of 448th Bomb Group Commander Col. James Thompson: http://www.taracopp.com/8th-Air-Force- 448th-Bomb-Group/04011044/i-C5Wv8xx/XL

c. Dog tags: http://www.taracopp.com/8th-Air-Force- 448th-Bomb-Group/04011044/i-VNZVWdQ/XL

66) Ploesti's defenses: "Air Power in the Mediterranean," Officer of the Commander-in-Chief, Mediterranean Allied Air Forces, 27 Feb. 1945, at: http://www.znaci.net/00002/315.pdf

Chapter 16: A Triangle and an Upside-down "T"

67) The 98th's Aug. 1, 1943 mission against Ploesti, Romania, is based off of the mission reports, interrogation reports, photographs and maps preserved by the National Archives and found here: http://www.taracopp.com/98th-Bombardment-Group-WWII/August-1-1943-Ploesti-Mission/ and also found here: http://www.taracopp.com/98th-Bombardment- Group-WWII/Ploesti-Still-Photos/

Chapter 17: June 6, 1944

70) Description of Terry taken from the official U.S. Army Air Forces crew photo of Plane 5, 506th Parachute Infantry Regiment, Pathfinder Unit, provided courtesy of Pathfinder historian Dave Berry.

71 Re-creation of the hours and days before the jump is based on the memoirs of George Goodridge, 506th Parachute Infantry Regiment, Fox Company, "The Airborne Invasion of Normandy," a chapter from "Toccoa to Normandy to Berchtesgaden, A Proposed History of Fighting Fox Company," preserved at the National Archives and found here: http://www.taracopp.com/-

Pathfinders/506th-PIR-Fox-Company-George/

72) Additional details on the hours before the mission were found in 506th Parachute Infantry Regiment James

73) E. Leach's report, "Operations of the 506th Parachute Infantry Regiment in the Invasion of Western Europe," http://www.taracopp.com/Pathfinders/Leach-summary- of-Normandy-drop/i-hQnvjmk/X3

74) The gold-winged torch: From the "Pathfinders" section of the In Memoriam website to U.S. Airborne paratroopers located at http://www.usairborne.be/Pathfinders/us_pathfinders.htm

75) Pre-operation preparations for the launch were also based on the IX Troop Carrier Command's History of its D-Day operations, "H-Hour Minus Four-and-a-Half," by Captain Luther Davis, and found here: http://www.taracopp.com/Pathfinders/IX-Troop-Carrier-Command-Unit/98th Launch from Lecce to Ploesti

76) Pre-mission briefing and time of departure: "Special Narrative Report No. 60, Mission 6 June 1944 - Romana- Americana Oil Refinery, Ploesti, Roumania," found here: http://www.taracopp.com/98th-Bombardment-Group- WWII/X-06061944/i-LjgtJH7/A

77) History of "Operation Tidal Wave" and subsequent launches, including all statistics on sorties flown and aircraft lost are pulled from "Air Power in the Mediterranean," Officer of the Commander-in-Chief, Mediterranean Allied Air Forces, 27 Feb. 1945, accessed online at: http://www.znaci.net/00002/315.pdf: and the Air Force Historical Support Division, Ploesti fact sheets, accessed online at http://www.afhso.af.mil/topics/factsheets/factsheet.asp?id=17993; and "The Air Force Story," Ploesti March 1944 to August 1944 https://archive.org/details/gov.dod.dimoc.26158

78) The memories of how the men reacted to the stress of the bombing missions: The Memoirs of Col. Richard C. Harris.

79) The takeoff time of Plane 5 is located on its mission sheet for the June 6, 1944 mission: http://www.taracopp.com/Pathfinders/

80) What his equipment included: the memoirs of George Goodridge, 506th Parachute Infantry Regiment, Fox Company, "The Airborne Invasion of Normandy," found here: http://www.taracopp.com/Pathfinders/506th-PIR-Fox-Company-George/

81) The minutes before the drop are based on Goodridge's accounts and Jerome Priesler's "First to Jump, How the Band of Brothers was Aided by the Brave Paratroopers of Pathfinder Company," published by the Penguin Group.

82) Time of jump and altitude were recorded on the mission report sheet for Plane 5, found here: http://www.taracopp.com/Pathfinders/Flight-records-of-Pathfinder

83) The re-creation of the flight of Dick's B-24 toward Ploesti is based on the Narrative of his Distinguished Flying Cross, found here: http://www.taracopp.com/98th-Bombardment-Group-WWII/My-Grandfather-Richard-C/ Additional details are taken from The Memoirs of Col. Richard C. Harris

84) The records of the 98th Bomb Group's mission over Ploesti, found here, including the number of planes and the names of pilots involved: http://www.taracopp.com/98th-Bombardment-Group-WWII/X-06061944/i-LjgtJH7/A and http://www.taracopp.com/98th-Bombardment-Group- WWII/X-06061944/

85) Lt.Plane hearing of "strange B-24" found here: http://www.tara-copp.com/98th-Bombardment-Group- WWII/X-06061944/i- wv4nbzk/A

86) Maj. Bill Sawyer in the air: http://www.taracopp.com/98th-

Bombardment-Group-WWII/X-06061944/i-cbMhvzg/A

87) Report of D-Day Pathfinder Activities, 1 July, 1944, Capt. Frank Lillyman, 502nd Parachute Infantry Regiment, 101st Airborne Division Pathfinder Officer, found here: http://www.6juin1944.com/assaut/aeropus/en_page.php? page=af-ter_pathf_101

88) 506th Parachute Infantry Regiment in Normandy Drop, as photographed at the National Archives: http://www.tara-copp.com/Pathfinders/Carentan/

89) Terry's narrative of reassembling in the dark is based off of the Leach and Goodridge reports, the accounts in Jerome Priesler's "First to Jump," and the accounts of the East Company men interviewed in Marcus Brotherton's "Who We are Alive and Remain," and "A Company of Heroes."

90) The letter by Burr Smith to Annette was provided courtesy of Smith's daughter, Susan Smith Finn.

91) Carentan geographic descriptions and hazards are found in Regimental Unit Study No. 1, "The Carentan Causeway Fight," from the 502nd Parachute Infantry Regiment records at the National Archives and located here: http://www.taracopp.com/Pathfinders/Carentan-addtlfile/ and http://www.taracopp.com/Pathfinders/Carentan

92) The injuries that Terry sustained leading to his death, and the artifacts found on his body when he died are based on the 52-page report that comprises his Individual Deceased Personnel File, as provided by the U.S. Army Human Resources Command and located here: http://www.taracopp.com/Pathfind-ers/SSgt-Terrence-Salty-Harris/

93) Terry's death record: QMC Form No. 2, "Weekly Report of Burials No. 97. Aug. 30, 1944, entry No. 1643. Online at: http://www.taracopp.com/Pathfinders/SSgt-Terrence- Salty-

Harris/i-jhKfwdc/XL

Chapter 18: Resolution

95) Lt. Donald D. Pucket's Medal of Honor mission was based on the records of the National Archives for his July 9, 1944 flight over Ploesti, found here: http://www.taracopp.com/98th-Bombardment-Group-WWII/Pucket-Medal-of-Honor-Mis-sion

96) Lt. Sidney Paisner's notes on the Pucket crash: http://www.taracopp.com/98th-Bombardment-Group- WWII/Pucket-Medal-of-Honor-Mission/i-pxK2jH3/A

97) Crew scared to jump: http://www.taracopp.com/98th-Bombardment-Group-WWII/Pucket-Medal-of-Honor-Mission/i-gtkMf44/A and http://www.taracopp.com/98th-Bombardment- Group-WWII/Pucket-Medal-of-Honor-Mission/i-F2rwZg3/L
and http://www.taracopp.com/98th- Bombardment-Group-WWII/Pucket-Medal-of-Honor- Mission/i-nqHb3H5/L

98) Pucket's last words: http://www.taracopp.com/98th-Bombardment-Group-WWII/Pucket-Medal-of-Honor-Mission/i- FNJf3Mk/X3

99) Pucket name misspelled: http://www.taracopp.com/98th-Bombardment-Group-WWII/Pucket-Medal-of-Honor-Mission/i- QMC3S62/A

100) The letter from Col. Bill Sawyer on the occasion of Dick's death was provided by the late Mónica Lahtz Harris, my grandmother.

101) Dick's first dance with my grandmother was based on
The Memoirs of Col. Richard C. Harris, in his second "Chapter One."

Made in the USA
Lexington, KY
22 April 2019